More Praise for *Unlimited Sales Success* . . .

"Brian Tracy is a global authority in all areas of professional and personal development. Through the decades he has remained at the very top of the leader board. No one knows more about every aspect of the sale process, and in this splendid book he illustrates why he is the salesmaster and consummate hands-on teacher in life's most important art—the art of positive persuasion."

—Denis Waitley, author, *Being the Best*

"Brian Tracy hits another home run! Don't make a pitch without reading this first. Consume every morsel of insight and watch your sales soar!"

—Mark C. Thompson, *New York Times* bestselling
author of *Admired: 21 Ways to Double Your Value*

"Brian Tracy has written yet another incredible book . . . If you're in sales and want to achieve greater results and make more money, read this book."

—Laura Stack, author of *Execution IS the Strategy*
and *What to Do When There's Too Much to Do*

"Brian Tracy's new book on sales will help you shape your future for unlimited success in the most exciting career you can choose and excel in. A must read; a vital addition to your library. Buy it, read it, study it, and apply its wisdom and truths. This book is essential for your long-term success."

—Dr. Peter Legge, OBC, LL.D., D. Tech. Chairman
and CEO, Canada Wide Media Limited

UNLIMITED SALES SUCCESS

12 SIMPLE STEPS FOR SELLING MORE THAN YOU EVER THOUGHT POSSIBLE

BRIAN TRACY

AND

MICHAEL TRACY

AMACOM AMERICAN MANAGEMENT ASSOCIATION
NEW YORK · ATLANTA · BRUSSELS · CHICAGO · MEXICO CITY
SAN FRANCISCO · SHANGHAI · TOKYO · TORONTO · WASHINGTON, D.C.

Bulk discounts available. For details visit:
www.amacombooks.org/go/specialsales
Or contact special sales:
Phone: 800-250-5308 / E-mail: specialsls@amanet.org
View all the AMACOM titles at: www.amacombooks.org

This publication is designed to provide accurate and authoritative information in regard to the subject matter covered. It is sold with the understanding that the publisher is not engaged in rendering legal, accounting, or other professional service. If legal advice or other expert assistance is required, the services of a competent professional person should be sought.

Library of Congress Cataloging-in-Publication Data

Tracy, Brian.
Unlimited sales success : 12 simple steps for selling more than you ever thought possible / Brian Tracy and Michael Tracy.
    pages cm
Includes index.
ISBN 978-0-8144-3324-9 — ISBN 0-8144-3324-3 1. Selling. I. Title.
HF5438.25.T136 2014
658.85—dc23
                                                        2013024854

About AMA
American Management Association (www.amanet.org) is a world leader in talent development, advancing the skills of individuals to drive business success. Our mission is to support the goals of individuals and organizations through a complete range of products and services, including classroom and virtual seminars, webcasts, webinars, podcasts, conferences, corporate and government solutions, business books, and research. AMA's approach to improving performance combines experiential learning—learning through doing—with opportunities for ongoing professional growth at every step of one's career journey.

Printing number
10 9 8 7 6 5 4 3 2 1

CONTENTS

UNLIMITED SALES SUCCESS

THE NEW REALITIES
OF SELLING

Your present circumstances don't determine where
you can go; they merely determine where you start.
—Nido Qubein

WELCOME TO THE new world of selling! More people are going to make more money and enjoy greater financial success in the months and years ahead in the profession of selling than ever before. Fully 5 percent of self-made millionaires are salespeople who started at the bottom, became very good in their field, earned high incomes, and became wealthy. And what hundreds of thousands, even millions, of other people have done, you can do as well. You just need to learn how.

My son Michael and I have condensed into this book everything we have learned from our experience selling millions of dollars of products and services. Everything in these pages is time-tested, proven, and practical, and designed to help you make faster and easier sales in any market.

When I began my sales career, I knew nothing of the skills and techniques you are about to learn. I did not graduate from high school. I worked at laboring jobs for several years. When I could no longer find a laboring job, in desperation, I got into straight commission sales, cold-calling one office after another in the day-time and houses and apartments in the evenings.

I got the three-part sales training program that is common worldwide: "Here are your cards, here are your brochures, there's the door."

If I didn't sell, I didn't eat. I got up every morning at six and was waiting in the parking lot when people came to work at eight o'clock. My sales results were terrible. I was making just enough sales to eat and to pay for a small room in a boardinghouse. I had holes in my shoes, empty pockets, and no future.

A Life-Changing Event

Then I did something that changed my life. I went to the top sales-man in our office, a man a few years older than me who was selling ten times as much as anyone else. And he wasn't even working very hard! He always had a pocketful of money. He went to nice restaurants and nightclubs. He drove a new car and lived in a beautiful apartment.

I took a deep breath and went up to him and asked him out-right, "What are you doing differently? How is it that you are making so many more sales than me, or anyone else?"

He looked at me with surprise and then said, "Well, if you want some help, show me your sales presentation and I will cri-tique it for you."

Now, I admitted that I had heard there was such a thing as a "sales presentation." But it was like the far side of the moon, something

I had never actually seen in reality. I told the top salesman that when I called on customers, I simply said whatever fell out of my mouth.

He said, "No. No. No. Selling is a profession. It is both a science and an art. It follows a logical, orderly process from the first step through to the closing of the sale and the satisfied customer. Let me give you an example of a sales presentation."

He then sat me down and asked me questions, commenting as he went along, exactly as if I were a prospective customer for our product. Instead of talking continually, as I did when I got in front of a prospect, he asked questions in a logical sequence, leading from the general to the particular, from qualifying me as a prospect through to closing the sale. It was different from anything I had ever experienced.

From that day forward, instead of talking continually, I asked better questions of my potential customers and listened closely to their answers. And my customers reacted to me differently. And I started to make sales, and then more and more sales. I began reading books on selling and listening to audio programs. I began attending every sales seminar I could find. And each time I learned and applied something new, my sales went up, and up, and up. Within a year, I was earning ten times as much income. My whole life changed forever.

What I discovered was the oldest of laws: the Law of Cause and Effect. This law says that for every effect in your life, there is a cause, or a series of causes. If there is any effect that you would like to have in your life, find others who have already achieved that outcome and then do the same things that they did to get there.

In my sales seminars, I often start off by asking, "How many people here would like to double their income in the next year or so?"

Every hand in the room goes up. I then explain that if you want to double your income, it is not that difficult. You simply identify some people who are earning twice as much as you—and who, by definition, at one time were earning half as much as you are today—and then you find out what they did to get from where they were to where they are today. Then, if you do the same things that other successful people do, you soon get the same results. It is not a miracle. It is not a matter of luck. It is simply a matter of law—the Law of Cause and Effect.

Selling in the Markets of Today and Tomorrow

Since that day in my early twenties, when I first learned how to make more sales, I have started, built, managed, or turned around twenty-two companies. I have recruited, trained, managed, and personally motivated hundreds of salespeople in different sales organizations. I have personally trained more than 2 million salespeople in sixty-one countries around the world. Many thousands of my graduates have gone from rags to riches, from the bottom to the top. Many have become millionaires and multimillionaires, actually ending up owning the companies that they were working for when they started using the ideas that you will learn in this book.

The good news is that sales success is quite predictable. When you do what other successful people do, you will soon get the same results that they do.

The first step is to understand the most important factors that determine sales success or failure in today's market. It seems that in every market, selling every product and service, in every industry, there are salespeople who continue to grow and prosper in sales, earning a wonderful living for themselves and providing well for their families.

How do they do it? They know that change is taking place faster today in every industry than ever before. Because of ever-greater competition, the need to please ever-more-demanding customers, increasing price sensitivity to products and services, and incredible uncertainty in national and international markets, the companies and individuals who survive and thrive are those that are fast and flexible in rapidly changing conditions.

Charles Darwin wrote that "survival goes not to the strongest or most intelligent, but to the one who is most adaptable to change." The marketplace has changed dramatically, and continues to change, and you must change with it.

The Seven New Realities

Specifically, there are seven new realities, or facts, that you must incorporate into your thinking and your actions to achieve the kind of sales results and income that are truly possible for you. Today, more than ever before:

1. There are more sellers than buyers in every field.

2. Selling is more complex.

3. Selling requires greater focus and clarity.

4. Selling requires greater preparation.

5. Customers are more demanding.

6. Sales success requires multiple calls.

7. Closing the sale is harder.

THERE ARE MORE SELLERS THAN BUYERS IN EVERY FIELD

The first new reality is that, in every field today, there are more sellers than buyers. The competition is more fierce and determined than ever before. There are fewer customer dollars available for an ever-expanding and desirable assortment of products and services. And whatever got you to where you are today is not enough to keep you there—or to get you any farther.

SELLING IS MORE COMPLEX

Second, selling is more complex than it was in the past. Product and service offerings, prices, and company capabilities are more complex than ever. Customer needs, wants, desires, and problems are more complex. Multiple customer contacts and meetings are required to make a sale today. And if anything, selling is going to become even more complex and demanding in the future. You are going to have to run faster just to stay in the same place.

CLARITY IS ESSENTIAL

The third new reality is that selling requires greater focus and clarity than ever before. You must develop absolute clarity about your ideal customer—that is, the person who can and will buy your product or service in the shortest period of time. You cannot afford to spend time speaking to people who cannot or will not buy what you are selling.

Once you have thought through and identified your ideal customer, you must then ask, "Why would your ideal customer buy from you rather than from your competitors?" What is your competitive advantage?

In 2012 alone, large and small companies spent more than $8 billion on market research in a variety of attempts to answer these questions. The greater clarity you have about the perfect customer for you and your product or service, the more of these perfect customers you will find, and the faster you will recognize them when you come across them. Focus and concentration on your very best potential customer is the key to your getting into the top 20 percent of money earners and moving up from there.

CREDIBILITY MEANS BEING PREPARED

Fourth, it's a fact that selling today requires greater preparation. It is absolutely essential that you do your homework on customers before you call on them for the first time. Fortunately, with Google and other online search engines, you can do better and faster research on people and corporations than ever before in human history. With a few mouse clicks, you can have access to information that used to require hours of research at the local library to uncover.

Sometimes I ask my audiences, "What is the single most important factor in selling today? What is the one factor that determines how much you sell, how fast you sell it, how much you earn, the size of your bank account, the home you live in, the quality of your life, and everything that happens to you personally and financially? What is the one factor?"

And the answer is, "Credibility!" Your credibility with the customer is more important than any other factor. The more the customer trusts you and believes you, the lower the customer's fear of making a buying mistake. The more the customer trusts you, the easier it is for that customer to buy from you. In fact, when your credibility level is high enough, the customer will buy from you and not even ask the price.

And the better prepared you are, the greater is your credibility from the first meeting. Do some "pre-call preparation." Find out everything you possibly can about your customers before you meet with them for the first time. When you meet with prospects and you explain how impressed you are with their accomplishments, and you can mention some background detail on the individual and the organization, your credibility will soar. The customer will be more open and interested in talking to you because you have obviously done your homework.

Also, before the call, think through and plan exactly what you are going to do and what you want to accomplish in the sales call. The better prepared you are in setting your pre-call objectives, the more focused and clear you will be when it comes to asking questions and having a conversation, and the more impressive you will look and sound to your prospective customer.

Finally, quickly write down everything that was discussed in the call immediately after you get out of the presence of the prospect. When you walk into a second or third meeting fully prepared because you have carefully reviewed your notes from the previous meetings, you look and sound like a professional. Your credibility goes straight up.

The final benefit to preparation, aside from building your credibility quickly from the first call, is that it gives you a tremendous sense of self-confidence. And self-confidence is a vital psychological ingredient in successful selling.

CUSTOMERS ARE MORE DEMANDING

A fifth reality is that customers are more demanding nowadays. Why? Because they can be! And if anything, they are going to be more demanding in the weeks and months ahead.

Customers today are more skeptical and suspicious because of their previous buying experiences. They are afraid of buying the wrong product, paying too much, receiving too little, and being left in the lurch after the sale, as has happened to them in the past.

Customers also receive multiple offers of products and services. Your competitors are calling on them continuously. In their spare moments, your customers can go onto the Internet and find every variation of your product or service that is available in the world today, and at the lowest possible prices.

It used to be that the salesperson was the expert when he called on a prospect. He knew more about his product or service, and the competitors in the market, than the customer. Today, the roles are reversed. Customers know as much or more than the salesperson, and what they don't know, they can find out in a few seconds.

Finally, customers are more demanding because they have limited resources. They do not have the kind of money that makes it possible for them to make a buying mistake. As a result, they proceed more slowly. They question every claim you make. They compare your offer with those of your competitors. They procrastinate and delay making any buying decision.

MULTIPLE-CALL SELLING

The sixth new reality is that it takes multiple calls to make a sale. When I started off, calling from door to door, it was a single-call selling process. I would meet a prospect, ask qualifying questions, make my sales pitch, and ask for a buying decision. The size of my product was small and the risk of making a poor decision was low.

Today, however, because of the incredible complexity of the modern market and the level of competition in the marketplace, you have to make an average of four or five calls on a qualified prospect to actually make a sale, and at each one of these meetings, the sales process can stop because of a new piece of information.

Your first call may be just to start a relationship, and to discover if a need for your product or service actually exists. The purpose of the first call is to separate prospects from suspects. The second and third calls may be to get more information, to make a presentation, or to present a proposal. The fourth and fifth meetings with the prospect may be to negotiate, finalize the purchase agreement, and close the sale.

The best sales organizations and salespeople use what is called the "milestone method" of selling. They carefully note the stage to which the sale has developed, knowing that for a certain number of prospects who begin the process, a specific percentage will actually become customers at the end of the process.

The question is, Where are you in the sales process? Is this your first meeting? Is this your second or third meeting? How far along are you toward actually making the sale and collecting payment?

CLOSING THE SALE

Closing the sale is harder today than it used to be, which is the seventh new reality of sales. Customers have fewer resources and are reluctant to change or try something new. Even if your product or service is attractive, the customer has to move out of her comfort zone and "stretch" before she is willing to begin using something new or different. In addition, there are "switching costs," which can be mental, physical, and financial. Sometimes, from the customer's point of view, it is just too much trouble to purchase your product or service.

There are other reasons why closing the sale is more difficult than ever before. We call these the "rules." The first rule is, "No authority? No sale!" What this means is that if the person you are talking to does not have the authority to make the buying decision, he has no choice but to put you off by saying, "Let me think it over."

The second rule: "No money? No sale!" If their financial situation is such that your prospects simply cannot afford your product or service, then no matter how attractive it is, or how good it could be for the prospect, no sale can take place.

The third rule is, "No need? No sale!" A major reason qualified prospects do not buy a product is because they do not fully understand or appreciate how much better off their life and work could be if they had your product. Either you have not increased the intensity of their buying desire and made the product or service compelling enough, or the customer feels that the increment in value is too small to justify the time and expense of buying what you are selling.

The final rule: "No urgency? No sale!" Because customers are fearful about making a wrong buying decision, if they can possibly delay the decision, they will. This is why you should always have an "extra reason" for the customer to buy today rather than putting off the purchase until a later time. Sometimes we call this a "kicker." You can offer free delivery, extra services, special discounts or rebates, or greater speed of delivery. But you should always have something in your back pocket that you can pull out at the end of the sales conversation to encourage the customer to buy immediately.

These are some of the new realities of selling. They are not personal. Every salesperson selling virtually every product or service in the market today faces these same realities. They are facts of life. As the Marines say, "Adapt! Adjust! Respond!"

Learn What You Have to Learn

Your job is to learn what you have to learn, and do what you have to do, to become one of the most successful and highest-paid sales professionals in your field. Fortunately, the answers have all been found. There are no secrets. Your job is to do what other top-performing salespeople do, over and over again, until you master the same skills. The good news is that you'll start getting improved sales results from the first day that you apply these practical, proven ideas.

ACTION EXERCISES

1. What are the major factors in our fast-paced world that are affecting your sales today?

2. What will you need to start doing, or do more of, to succeed in the markets of tomorrow?

3. What are some of the biggest changes in customers and product/service offerings affecting your sales?

4. What are three qualities or characteristics of the ideal customer for the product or service you sell?

5. What are the most important things you need to learn about your customers before you can call on them?

6. Why don't qualified customers buy from you? What holds them back?

7. What can you do to create a sense of urgency in your prospects to encourage them to make the buying decision immediately?

And finally, what one action are you going to take as a result of what you have learned in this book introduction?

THE PSYCHOLOGY
OF SELLING

*Ambition is the spur that makes men struggle with
destiny. It is heaven's own incentive to make
purpose great and achievement greater.*
—Donald G. Mitchell

WHY ARE SOME salespeople more successful than others?

When I started in selling many years ago, I struggled for
months, barely earning enough to survive while all around me
other salespeople were selling and earning much more than me,
and they didn't seem to be any smarter or working any harder.

My first breakthrough was the discovery of the 80/20 rule. It
says that 20 percent of the salespeople make 80 percent of the
sales and earn 80 percent of the money. That means the average
income of the people in the top 20 percent is sixteen times the
average income of the people in the bottom 80 percent.

When I first heard that statistic, I was both inspired and discouraged. I was discouraged because I had never been good at anything in my life, let alone been in the top 20 percent. I failed school, worked at laboring jobs, and often slept on the ground with everything I owned in a backpack that I carried with me. The idea of being in the top 20 percent was exciting but overwhelming. I just did not think it could be possible for me.

Then I learned another fact: Every person in the top 20 percent started in the bottom 20 percent. Everyone who is doing well today was once doing poorly. Everyone at the front of the line of life started at the back of the line. As T. Harv Eker says, "Every master was once a disaster."

I immediately made a decision to be in the top 20 percent. I learned later that making a decision, of any kind, and then taking action on that decision, is often the turning point in your life. Without a decision to be in the top 20 percent, it simply will not happen. You will not get to the top of your field as a matter of luck or chance. People who get to the top of any field get there after they make a decision, and then they back up that decision with hard, hard work, month after month and year after year, until they make their decision a reality.

In his book *Outliers*, Malcolm Gladwell reports on research that says it takes about seven years and/or 10,000 hours of dedication and hard work to get to the top of your field. This doesn't just mean that you go to work and come home each day for seven years. It means that you throw your whole heart into becoming better and better, like a person running a sprint in a big race, and you work your heart out to develop your skills.

In his work on "deliberate practice," Anders Ericsson at the University of Florida concludes that the people who get to the top invest ten years of hard work to achieve "elite performance."

When I share these statistics with my audiences, there is often a big moan from the salespeople present. They say, "But I am thirty years old today. You are saying that it will take me seven to ten years to get to the top of my field. I have to wait to be seven to ten years older."

This is true. But then I ask, "How much older will you be in seven to ten years, in any case?"

The fact is that *time is going to pass anyway*. Seven years from now, you will be seven years older. The only question is whether you will be at the top of your field and one of the highest-paid people in the industry. And this is almost totally a matter of personal choice.

Remember, you can learn any skill you need to learn in order to achieve any goal you can set for yourself. All sales skills are *learnable*. Everyone who is good at a particular skill today at one time could not do it at all. Many of the best salespeople I know were terrible at selling when they began, and terrified of prospecting, to boot. Today, however, they are some of the most positive and confident and highest-paid people in our society. And what they have done, you can do as well.

Self-Confidence and Self-Esteem

Just as 20 percent of salespeople make 80 percent of the sales and earn 80 percent of the money, the 80/20 rule also applies to individuals in a different way. It says that 80 percent of success is mental and emotional, not technical and physical.

The most important determinant of sales success in any field, in any economy, in any market, with any product or service, is self-confidence. When you have an unshakable belief in yourself and your ability to succeed, you become unstoppable, like a force of nature. The higher your level of self-confidence, the bigger the goals you will set for yourself, the faster you will bounce back from rejection and disappointment, and the more you will achieve in a shorter period of time.

What I also discovered was that self-confidence is determined by your self-esteem. Your self-esteem can be defined as "how much you like yourself."

The more you like yourself, the more confidence you have. The more you like yourself, the more you like other people, including your customers. The more you like your customers, the more they like you right back, and are willing to buy from you, and recommend you to their friends.

The flip side of self-esteem is called "self-efficacy." Self-efficacy is defined as how good you are at what you do. The more you like yourself, the better you do your work. The better you do your work, the more you like yourself. One hand washes the other. Self-esteem and self-efficacy reinforce each other.

Psychologists will say that everything you do in life affects your self-esteem in some way. Almost everything you do is to either build your self-esteem or protect it from being diminished by other people or circumstances. Your self-esteem is the "reactor core" of your personality that determines your levels of optimism, self-respect, and personal pride.

Everything you do to build your self-esteem also builds your self-confidence. When you truly like yourself or *love* yourself, and see yourself as a valuable and important person, you become more positive and cheerful and completely unafraid to call on customers and ask them to buy from you.

Seven Steps to Mental Fitness

Your level of self-esteem is your level of "mental fitness." Mental fitness can be compared to physical fitness. Just as you become physically fit by doing a series of workouts, you become mentally fit by exercising *mentally* in a series of ways. For you to develop high levels of self-confidence and self-esteem in selling, you must learn to think and act like the most positive and successful salespeople until your self-confidence becomes so high that you become unstoppable.

People with high self-esteem can sell well in any market. People with low self-esteem cannot sell even in the very best of markets. Self-esteem is the key.

There are seven steps to mental fitness in selling and for improving how you think and feel about yourself and your potential. To become a top salesperson you must be:

1. Ambitious

2. Courageous

3. Committed to your work

4. Professional

5. Responsible

6. Thoroughly prepared for each call

7. A continuous learner

By practicing each of these principles over and over, you will eventually get into the "mental Olympics" of selling.

TOP SALESPEOPLE ARE AMBITIOUS

They have an intense desire to be successful in selling. This is perhaps the most important quality of all for success in selling, or in any other field. After twenty-two years of studying the most successful people in America, Napoleon Hill concluded that "burning desire" was the starting point of all success and all riches. This has never changed throughout history.

My friend Les Brown says, "If you want to be successful, you have got to be hungry!"

If you are ambitious and determined enough to achieve your goals and be successful, nothing can really stop you. You must have high levels of ambition to succeed in selling because of the tremendous amount of failure and rejection that you will experience in calling on new people, making sales presentations, and asking them to buy.

Ambition is the fuel in the furnace of achievement. The more ambition and drive you have, the more you will roll over the speed bumps of life. The more ambitious you are, the faster you will bounce back from disappointment. The more ambitious you are, the more you will "keep on keeping on" until you finally achieve your goals.

Resolve to Be the Best. Because of their ambition, top salespeople are determined to be the best in their fields. As it happens, selling is a "default profession." This means that people do not grow up with a plan to enter the field of selling. Rather, it is something that they get into when they have no other choice or when nothing else works out for them. They get a sales job.

Eighty percent of people who start off in sales look upon it as an interim occupation. They are constantly looking around for something else to do. As a result, they never throw their whole hearts into selling. They never become excellent at selling, and they never succeed greatly. They tread water for most of their sales careers.

But the top people are different. They get into sales, usually accidentally, then at a certain point, something wonderful occurs to them. A light goes on. They look around them in their sales field and see that by becoming good at selling, they can achieve all of their goals. If they become the best in this profession, they can earn more money than professionals with many years of university education.

At this moment, their afterburners kick in. They make a decision to be the best in selling. They throw their whole hearts into learning, listening, and attending courses. And each time they learn and apply a new idea, their sales results improve. This in turn fuels their ambition and increases their determination to succeed.

Here is one of the great discoveries: Anything less than a commitment to excellence is an acceptance of mediocrity. Excellence or elite performance in your field is the result of many years of hard, hard work on self-improvement. Just as the average athlete who makes it to the Olympics has been training for seven to ten years, the average salesperson who reaches the top of his field has been working on himself for seven to ten years.

Earl Nightingale wrote, "Happiness is the progressive realization of a worthy goal or ideal." When you commit to excellence, to being the best in your field, and you work on improving yourself every single day, you will begin to see results almost immediately.

Your level of ambition and your determination to be the best in your field is the nitroglycerin that causes your potential to explode over time.

TOP SALESPEOPLE ARE COURAGEOUS

They continually confront the fears that hold most people back. If ambition is the driving force of success, then courage is the way to unlock ambition because fear is the major obstacle to success.

When I began studying the psychology of high performance, I was amazed to discover that *fear of failure* is the biggest single obstacle to success and happiness in adult life. It is not failure. Everyone fails over and over. It is instead the thought or fear of failure that paralyzes performance.

Fear of failure of any kind, even if imaginary, acts as a brake on your potential. It stops you from taking action. Fear of failure causes you to procrastinate, delay, and avoid any situation where you may not succeed, especially sales situations.

Ralph Waldo Emerson once wrote about an experience that changed his life. He was walking down the street as a ten-year-old boy in Concord, Massachusetts, when a piece of paper blew against his leg. On the piece of paper it said, "If you would be successful in life, make a habit of doing the things you fear. If you do the thing you fear, the death of fear is certain."

His life was never the same after that. And your life can change dramatically as well when you also make a habit of doing the things you fear, until the death of fear is certain.

Glenn Ford wrote that "if you do not do the thing you fear, the fear controls your life."

The fact is that it is impossible to succeed without failing. Top people fail more often than average or unsuccessful people. Top people do not like to fail, but they realize that it is impossible to achieve their goals unless they are willing to fail over and over again on the journey.

Just as you become what you think about most of the time, it is also true that you become what you *say to yourself* most of the time. There are four magic words that you can repeat, over and over, to build your self-confidence and lower the fear of failure. They are: "I can do it! I can do it! I can do it!"

Whenever you are hesitating to step out and do something that you fear, you can neutralize that emotion long enough to take action by emphatically repeating those words: "I can do it!"

Conquer the Fear of Rejection. The second major fear that sabotages your success, especially in selling, is the fear of rejection. This fear comes from early childhood experiences where we were criticized and we were the victims of "conditional love" from our parents. It is said that all emotional problems in adult life stem from "love withheld" in childhood. If you were raised in an environment that was not encouraging and supportive, you can reach adulthood with tremendous feelings of insecurity and even hypersensitivity, such that you are negatively affected by the thoughts, opinions, and attitudes of others, whether real or imagined.

In sales, fear of rejection is sometimes referred to as "call reluctance," and it is the greatest obstacle to sales success. Unless you can overcome this fear of rejection, it is impossible for you to fulfill your true potential as a sales professional.

Fortunately, you can deliberately play tricks on your mind. You can actually reprogram yourself so that instead of fearing rejection, you actually look forward to it. You can hardly wait to get up and get rejected each morning.

When I started off selling, knocking on doors, I would create every excuse not to risk the rejection that I knew I was going to get from the first call in the morning. Then I learned something that changed my sales career: Rejection is not personal. You are probably thinking, "What? Do you mean that when a person rejects my offering of a product or service, it has nothing to do with me? It is a completely impersonal response to a commercial offer in a competitive society?" Yes!

When you call on new prospects and they respond in a negative way, it says nothing about your true value or self-worth. The prospect you are calling on doesn't even know who you are or anything about you. The rejection is completely impersonal, neutral, and not aimed at you at all.

As soon as I learned this truth, my sales activity increased significantly. I would get up every morning and I would say to myself: "Today I am going to face a lot of rejection. But I am going to use every rejection as a spur to greater effort. Each time I get rejected, I will become more positive and more determined and more eager to call on more prospects than I was before!"

In no time, I was looking forward to my first rejection. I had preprogrammed my subconscious mind to respond with feelings of optimism and enthusiasm as soon as I got rejected. Sometimes, I would actually laugh out loud at the first rejection of the day, feeling that I was unstoppable.

TOP SALESPEOPLE ARE COMMITTED TO THEIR WORK

The most successful people in every field, including and especially sales, are totally committed to what they are doing. They put their whole hearts into their work and continually strive to do it well and to get better.

There is a direct relationship between how much you believe in the goodness and importance of what you are doing and how persuasive you are in presenting and selling your products to others. To start with, top salespeople *believe in their companies*. They believe that their companies are excellent organizations and they are proud to work for them.

Top salespeople *believe in their products and services*. They believe that the products and services they offer are the best in the market. They believe that their products and services can actually help people to improve their lives and work. They believe so much in their products that they use them themselves whenever possible, enthusiastically sell them to their family and friends, and speak highly about them whenever their products and services are discussed.

They *believe in their customers* and want to help them. Top salespeople see themselves as "helpers" and are always looking for ways to improve the lives of their customers with their products and services. Another vital part of commitment is that top salespeople care about their customers. The highest-paid sales professionals are emotionally involved with their products and services, on the one hand, and their customers, on the other. They deeply want to make a difference in the lives of their customers with what they sell.

Finally, top salespeople *believe in themselves* and their ability to succeed. They have an almost unshakable confidence in their ability to achieve their goals and to overcome obstacles. They are confident, positive, and irresistible.

TOP SALESPEOPLE ARE PROFESSIONALS

When I started out selling financial services, I put the words "Sales Representative" on my business cards. That was how I saw myself, and that was how my prospects and customers saw me as well.

Then one day, I decided to change the description of myself to "Consultant." I threw away my existing business cards and got new ones with the title "Financial Consultant" on the front of the card.

It was quite amazing! From that day forward, I thought of myself as a consultant: as a professional adviser, counselor, and guide to my clients in helping to organize their financial lives and investments. And my customers responded differently as well. When they saw the "Financial Consultant" title on my card, they treated me differently. Instead of being skeptical and suspicious, they were more open, inviting, and interested in what I had to say.

Become a Consultant. Top salespeople see themselves as consultants and advisers—not just as salespeople. How do you become a consultant? Simple. You behave like a consultant in every customer interaction. How do salespeople consult? They ask good questions and listen carefully to the answers. They seek to understand rather than to be understood. They focus intently on the customer and seek ways to understand the customer's situation so that they can make good recommendations to help the customer.

Consultative salespeople look for customer problems they can solve. They recognize that whatever they sell, it is a *solution* to a problem or need that the customer has. Their first job in the sales conversation is to uncover the true need and understand what is necessary to satisfy that need.

Consultants see themselves as working for the client, rather than for themselves. And the most interesting discovery is that customers will accept you at your own evaluation of yourself. If you see yourself and think about yourself as a consultant, and describe yourself as a consultant to your customers, they will accept that you are a consultant, and they will treat you accordingly.

Perhaps the hardest part of becoming a consultant rather than a salesperson is having the courage to call yourself a consultant for the first time. (For more on what it takes to be a consultant, see Chapter 5 on "Selling Consultatively.")

TOP SALESPEOPLE ARE RESPONSIBLE

The starting point of personal greatness is when you accept 100 percent responsibility for your life and for everything that happens to you. This is another area where the 80/20 rule comes into play. The top 20 percent of performers in every field see themselves as self-employed. They see themselves as being in charge of their own lives.

When you are self-employed, you see yourself as the president of a company with one employee—yourself. You are responsible for selling one product—your own personal services—into a competitive marketplace. (In the next chapter, I explain in more detail how to be president of You, Inc.)

Top salespeople see themselves as the presidents of their own personal sales corporation.

Top salespeople do not complain about anything, especially their company, the competition, or the challenges of selling in a tough market. Top salespeople do not criticize other people, especially their competitors. Top salespeople refuse to make excuses. Instead of making excuses, they make progress.

Especially, self-responsible professionals do not blame anything in their lives on anyone or anything else. They repeat the words, "I am responsible! I am responsible! I am responsible!" over and over again throughout the day.

Take Charge of Everything. As presidents of their own personal services corporations, top salespeople are in charge of every aspect of the business. They are in charge of goal setting and strategic planning. They are responsible for quality control and continuous improvement. They are responsible for marketing, sales, and income generation. They are responsible for their finances and for all of their activities. Especially, and most important, they are responsible for *results*.

Top salespeople accept responsibility for planning and organizing each day in advance. They recognize that the only product they have to sell is their own personal time, and they organize their days so that they maximize every minute they get in front of customers to explain their products and services.

Top salespeople are responsible for getting sales results, for achieving and surpassing their quotas, no matter what else is going on in the marketplace.

There seems to be a direct relationship between self-esteem and self-responsibility. The more responsibility you accept personally, the more powerful you feel, which heightens your self-esteem and self-confidence. The more you accept responsibility, the more positive you feel, and the more energy you have. The more energy you have, the more outwardly focused you are when it comes to getting busy and getting business results.

TOP SALESPEOPLE ARE THOROUGHLY PREPARED FOR EACH CALL

It seems that preparation is the mark of the true professional, in every field, especially sales. The more prepared you are before you meet with a customer, the greater your self-confidence and the better impression you make on the customer, especially in the first meeting.

As I described in the book's introduction, top salespeople learn everything they can about their customers before they call on them. They determine their goals for each call and write out the questions they intend to ask in advance. After each call, they write down every detail and keep accurate notes and records that they can refer to when they make subsequent calls.

One characteristic of top salespeople is that they do their planning and preparation before and after the sales day. They plan their week in advance on Saturday or Sunday. They plan every day the evening before or in the morning before the sales day begins. Planning and preparation is done "off-line." During the day, when customers are available to be seen, the real professional does nothing but visit customers.

TOP SALESPEOPLE ARE CONTINUOUS LEARNERS

The fact is that "to earn more, you must learn more." There seems to be a direct relationship between how much you learn about how to do your job better and the size and growth of your income.

You should spend thirty to sixty minutes each day reading sales books, preferably in the morning before you start out. Reading one or two chapters of a good sales book each morning translates into about one book a week, or fifty books a year. By reading regularly in your field, you will soon become one of the most knowledgeable and highest-paid salespeople in your industry.

When I discovered the incredible power of reading sales books early in my career, it transformed my life. When I have encouraged other salespeople to read each day, they have reported back to me immediate increases in their sales, sometimes doubling and tripling their sales in as little as a month or two. Try it yourself and see.

Top salespeople also listen to educational audio programs in their cars, on their iPods or smartphones, and when exercising. They never miss a chance to learn something valuable and useful that can help them in their careers. The highest-paid salespeople also attend additional courses and seminars in selling and in their business fields. They are lifelong learners, hungry for new information.

Here is an attitude that I developed early in my career that has been extremely helpful to me. I go about my days imagining that there is a precious piece of information or knowledge out there that, if I can find it, will significantly increase my sales and my income. With this attitude, I am continually looking, reading, listening, and asking questions, attending seminars and workshops, looking for the holy grail.

And do you know what happens? I am always finding valuable ideas and insights, even after many years of sales success, which can help me to be even more effective in finding better customers and convincing them that my product or service is the best choice for them.

The 80/20 rule applies in the area of continuous learning as well. It says that 80 percent of salespeople either have not been professionally trained, or if they were, they seldom make any effort to learn anything new for the rest of their careers. And their income reflects their lack of continuous learning. They are always in the bottom 80 percent. They always struggle and worry about money. They always envy the top salespeople. But they are not willing to do the hard, hard work of continuous learning, and as a result, their lives never get any better.

But for the top 20 percent, it is different. Remember that happiness is the progressive realization of a worthy goal or ideal. Each time that you learn and apply something new, you feel a sense of personal growth and forward momentum. Learning releases endorphins in your brain, chemicals that are called nature's "happy drug." As you learn and apply new ideas, you feel happier and more positive. You feel more in charge of your own life. You feel personally empowered. Your self-esteem and self-confidence increase. You like and respect yourself even more each time you acquire a new piece of information that you can use to improve the quality of your life and your results.

Saint Francis of Assisi once wrote, "It's heaven all the way to heaven." It is not just the accomplishment of a big goal that makes you happy, it is the step-by-step feeling of forward motion toward your goal that fills you with happiness and excitement. Each time you learn and apply a new idea, or even think about applying a new idea, you become happier and more confident in your abilities.

Invest in Yourself. Here is the key to maximizing your potential and your income: Invest 3 percent of your income in yourself for the rest of your career. Take it off the top. If you earn $50,000 per year, invest $1,500 each year so that you can get better at what you are doing to earn that money in the first place.

The payoff for investing in yourself is ten, twenty, or even fifty times your investment. It is the highest payoff that you can possibly get for any financial investment in your world. A top salesman came up to me at one of my seminars and said that he had invested $75 in my sales program *The Psychology of Selling* a year before. He was already highly paid and successful as a salesperson, but he was open to learning new ideas. Yet, because of that sales program, and the ideas that it contained that he had not been aware of, he increased his personal income by $75,000 in just over twelve months. That is a return on investment of more than 1,000 times from a single audio learning program. And I've heard variations on this story from thousands of the highest-paid sales professionals in every industry who've invested in books, audio programs, and seminars over the years. When you invest 3 percent of your income back into yourself on a regular basis, you will be astonished at the speed at which your sales and your income increase.

Of course, the flip side is also true. If you do not continually invest in yourself in order to get better and better at what you do, nothing will happen. Your income will remain flat or gradually decline. You will struggle and worry about money throughout your career. You will always be envious, if not jealous, of the top salespeople who make all the money, drive the new cars, and take beautiful vacations. Which person do you want to be?

The good news is that you have the ability right now to become one of the top salespeople in your industry. Everyone who is at the top today started at the bottom. But when you start to think and act like the top people, you will soon get the results that they do. And sometimes, you will get these extraordinary results far faster than you can imagine today.

When I was just beginning my sales career, I studied the expanded Psychology of Selling program repeatedly and absorbed its key methods, techniques, and strategies. The most difficult yet important thing I learned during my first year of painstaking application of these skills was how to experience repeated rejection.

Rejection acts like the focusing mechanism on a camera; the more you receive rejection, the more you start to understand yourself. Your own self-concept becomes clear. One mental technique that helped me was to imagine a master sculptor chipping away small pieces of a human-size marble block. Each rejection I received was equivalent to one piece of stone being chipped away, allowing the form underneath to emerge a little more, until a solid smooth form stood forth. That solid form represents your true personality and your ability to persist in the face of rejection. Eventually, facing and overcoming the fear of rejection will act as a fuel and a teacher that will make you unstoppable.

Above the Delphi oracle from ancient Greece is an inscription: "Man, know thyself." Repeated rejection may be the fastest means to help you to know yourself and find out what you are really made of inside.

—MT

ACTION EXERCISES

Now, here are some questions to ask and answer, based on what we've covered in this chapter:

1. Exactly why do you want to be one of the best salespeople in your industry? What difference will that make in your life?

2. How would you work differently in your sales activities if you were absolutely guaranteed great success?

3. What are your major sales and income goals right now? How much do you want to earn, and how much will you have to sell to earn that amount over the next year?

4. What are the features and benefits of what you sell that you personally like the most?

5. What benefits do your products and services bring to your customers that give you the greatest sense of pleasure and satisfaction?

6. How can you behave more like a consultant and less like a salesperson the next time you meet with a prospect or client?

7. What would you do differently each day if you owned 100 percent of your company and you were 100 percent responsible for sales results in your business?

And finally, what one action are you going to take immediately as a result of what you have learned in this chapter?

PERSONAL SALES PLANNING

BE THE CEO OF YOU, INC.

*Find something you love to do and you'll never have
to work a day in your life.*
—Harvey Mackay

THE TOP 20 PERCENT of salespeople in every industry earn vastly more than the bottom 80 percent. Your goal is to be among the top 20 percent, and then to continually increase your sales and personal income. In this chapter, you will learn how successful people accomplish far, far more than the average person by planning their goals and activities in advance.

What is the most important and highest-paid work that you do? The answer is: *thinking!* The quality of your thinking largely determines the quality of your life. The more accurately you think about yourself, your goals, and the activities necessary to accomplish them, the more successful you will be at everything you do.

Your Most Valuable Asset

What is your most valuable financial asset? It is your *earning ability*. Your ability to earn money can be defined as your ability to get results that people will pay you for. The difference between high performers and low performers is that high performers have developed high levels of earning ability and low performers have not.

Your earning ability today is the sum total result of all of your knowledge and experience, all of your education and training, all of your habits and skills, up to this date. The good news is that each of these capabilities can be increased and improved upon. You can increase your earning ability continually and throughout your career.

As with any asset, however, your earning ability can either appreciate or depreciate. For people in the top 20 percent, their earning ability is increasing at an average of about 11 percent per year (according to studies done at the University of Chicago). For people in the bottom 80 percent, their earning ability, if they remain employed, increases by about one percent per year, if that.

If your most valuable asset increases at an average of 11 percent per year, you will double your income in seven years, and then double it again and again. Over the course of your career, you will become one of the highest-paid people in our society.

But if your income is only increasing by one percent per year because you are doing nothing to increase your earning ability, it will take seventy-two years before your income doubles. And this is without considering inflation, unemployment, or disruptions in your industry or the economy.

Perhaps the most important difference in work life today, as compared with the past, is that each of us is totally in charge of our own career and financial future. As I said in the last chapter, you are the president of an entrepreneurial company with one employee—*yourself*. You are in charge of selling one product— your own personal services. Your main goal in your work life is to increase the quality and quantity of the services you sell so that you can increase your income and the quality of your life.

The worst mistake you can ever make is to think that you work for anyone else but yourself. You are the president of a company called You, Inc. You are the president of your own career, your own life, and your own future. You determine your own income over time by the things you do and by the things you fail to do.

It is very often the things you fail to do that have the greatest effect on your life. If you fail to plan your life and work every day and every hour, it will cost you in terms of results and earning ability. If you fail to organize and set priorities on what you do, it will hurt you. If you do not continually upgrade your knowledge and skills, getting better and better, making your earning ability an appreciating asset, it is going to have a major negative impact on your life and your future.

Your Most Precious Resource

What is your most precious resource? Answer: *your time!* When you begin your career, if you are like most people, you have little or no money, but lots of time. You go into the marketplace and trade your services for money. If you are a good trader, your income will increase more and more as the years go by.

At the end of your career, you will have less time, but you should have a substantial amount of money accumulated. The worst thing that can happen to people is to work their whole lives, exchanging thirty or forty years of hard work, and to end up with not enough money to retire. Unfortunately, this is the situation for too many people today.

Personal Strategic Planning

The purpose of strategic planning for a business is to increase the return on equity (ROE), which is defined as "increasing the financial return on the actual amount of money invested in the business."

Your goal in *personal* strategic planning is also to increase your ROE. But in this sense, ROE stands for *return on energy*. This is your return on your "human capital." Your mental, emotional, and physical energy constitute your human capital, and it is all you really have to sell at the beginning of your career.

Your standard of living and your income are totally determined by how well you trade your personal energies in the marketplace for results and rewards. Unfortunately, most people never learn that their earning ability is their most precious and valuable financial asset. They take it for granted. They ignore it. They assume that it is something outside of their control. Most people use their time in a random and haphazard way. They get up in the morning, drink coffee, drive to work listening to the radio, chat with their coworkers, go out for coffee breaks and lunches, make a couple of sales calls, and then go home and watch television.

But that's not for you. Your life is too precious. Your goal is to live life to the fullest, to exchange every minute and every hour for the highest possible "return on energy."

Remember, you are your own boss. You decide your own income. You write your own paycheck. If you're not happy with your current income, go to the nearest mirror and negotiate with your boss. If you want more money, there is only one way that you can get it. It is by going out and making more and better sales. And this decision is largely under your control.

The GOSPA Strategy

In personal strategic planning, you always start with your goals—short-term, medium-term, and long-term goals. Where are you today? Where do you want to be in the future? And what steps will you have to take to get there?

A powerful way to help you think and make better decisions is for you to use the GOSPA (goals, objectives, strategies, plans, and activities) method of strategic thinking and planning:

▮ *Goals.* These are your long-term targets and desired outcomes. Setting goals begins with deciding exactly how much money you want to earn in the coming year. You can start by taking your highest gross income year to date and increasing it by 25 percent to 50 percent. If the most that you have ever earned in one year is $50,000, then you set a goal to earn $62,500 over the next twelve months. If you are more ambitious, you can set a goal to earn $75,000 over the next twelve months.

Once you have determined your annual income and sales goals, the next step is for you to break them down by month, week, and day. For example, if your annual income goal is $60,000, then your monthly income goal is $5,000. If your monthly income goal is $5,000, and you work fifty weeks per year, this means that you want to earn $1,200 each week. Earnings of $1,200 per week divided by five days equals $240 per day.

The final exercise, and perhaps the most important, is for you to determine your desired *hourly rate.* How much do you want or need to earn each hour in order to earn your daily income goal, your weekly income, and your annual income goal? If your annual income goal is $60,000, you divide this number by 2,000 hours (250 days times eight hours) to determine your desired hourly rate of $30. From this day forward, you refuse to do anything during the day that does not pay you $30 per hour or more.

▮ *Objectives.* The subgoals that you must accomplish on the way to achieving your long-term goals are your objectives. For example, you will have to call on a specific number of prospects in order to get a specific number of meetings that will turn into a specific number of presentations that will turn into a specific number of sales. A specific number of sales will turn into a specific amount of income.

In addition, among your objectives will be to develop excellent product knowledge and to improve your sales and time management skills. These are all essential objectives that you will have to accomplish in order to achieve your long-term income goal.

■ *Strategies.* These are the different ways that you can accomplish each of your objectives. For example, there are only three ways to increase sales:

1. Increase the number of transactions (make more individual sales).

2. Increase the size of each transaction (add-on, up-sell, cross-sell, and maximize the potential revenue from each sale).

3. Increase the frequency of transactions (do everything possible to get your customers to buy from you more often and give you recommendations and referrals to additional customers).

One of the best ways to determine your strategies for achieving an objective on the way to your goal is for you to make a list of everything that you can possibly do to achieve the subgoal. Organize the list in terms of value and priority. Decide exactly what you can do to increase your sales in one or more of these areas.

■ *Plans.* A plan is an organized list of activities to achieve the strategies in your plan. All top performers work from a list. They are continuous "list makers." Perhaps the best time management tool of all is a *checklist* that you create by writing down every step, in order, that you will have to take to achieve an objective on the way to your long-term goal. Once you have a checklist, you work on your list every day, accomplishing each task in order, until the larger goal is achieved.

▪ *Activities.* These are the daily actions that you take to carry out your plans, implement your strategies, achieve your objectives, and ultimately accomplish your goals. The better you think through each of these areas, the better results you will achieve, and the faster you will achieve them.

Control Your Activities

The key to sales success is for you to *control your activities* hour by hour and minute by minute. You have determined your annual income goal and the amount that you must sell in order to earn that income. Now you break the equation down into even smaller parts.

First, what is the average size of your sales? Good salespeople keep accurate records of their sales activities. They can tell you the average size of their sales on a month-by-month, year-by-year basis. They are very clear about how much they earn. They use this information as a baseline and continually work to improve their average income per sale.

What is the number of individual sales you will have to make in the course of a week, month, or year to achieve your desired annual income?

How many prospecting calls will you have to make? How many people will you need to contact initially to get the necessary number of appointments with interested prospects? You may have to make five, ten, or even twenty calls to get an appointment with an interested prospect. Keep accurate records.

How many presentations will you have to make to interested prospects to make the number of sales that you require to achieve your personal income goals? What is your closing ratio, per call, per presentation, per follow-up? Do you know how many people you have to talk to initially to get how many appointments, to make how many presentations, to make how many follow-ups, to make how many sales, and to earn how much per sale? By keeping accurate records, you will know the answers to these questions every day, every week, and every month.

You can accomplish more in a week or a month with a clear written plan than you can accomplish in a year or even two years without one. A personal strategic plan gives you a track to run on and ensures that you will accomplish more than you ever imagined possible. All top sales professionals work from a written plan. So should you.

Remember: Every minute you spend in planning will save approximately ten minutes in getting the results that are important to you. If you take ten minutes each day to plan, it will save you about one hundred minutes in the course of the day, a payoff of ten to one, or a 1,000 percent return on energy.

The Sales Funnel

Use the model of a sales funnel to plan your sales work and activities. There are several different parts of professional selling, but the "big three" are *prospecting*, *presenting*, and *following up and closing*.

Imagine a funnel that is wide at the top and narrow at the bottom. Your prospecting work fills the top of the funnel. You must put a lot of new prospects and suspects into the top of the funnel because only a few of them will move through the funnel and actually become customers.

The second main part of selling, and the second part of the funnel, is presenting your product or service as the best choice possible for this particular customer. (As you will learn later, the presentation is where the actual sale is made.) There is a direct ratio between the number of new prospects you speak with and the number of opportunities you will get to present your product or service. For this example, let us say that you need twenty prospects in the top of the funnel to get five presentations in the middle of the funnel.

The third part of the funnel, the narrowest part, is when you follow up and close the sale. If you must contact twenty prospects to get five presentations, out of those five presentations you may get two excellent potential customers to follow up with. From two potential customers you close one sale.

In this example, your sales ratio is 20:1. Once you have determined your current sales ratio, which will change with market conditions, personal experience, skill, and other factors, here is your strategy: Keep your funnel full. Continue to prospect, present, and follow up. And then commit yourself to getting better and better in each area.

Key Result Areas

There are seven key result areas in selling. All are essential for sales success. Your level of skill in each of these areas, on average, determines your income.

If you want to lose weight, the first thing that you do is stand on the scale and weigh yourself. This gives you your "baseline," which becomes your starting point. From this baseline you can compare your progress on a daily basis.

With your key result areas in selling, it is much the same. You start off by grading yourself on a scale of 1 to 10 in each of seven areas:

1. Prospecting

2. Building Rapport and Trust

3. Identifying Problems

4. Presenting Solutions

5. Answering Objectives

6. Closing the Sale

7. Resales and Referrals

The minimum skill level that you require for success is a grade of 7 or better. When you grade yourself on the following key result areas, be honest. You can only improve in an area after you admit that you are not as strong as you could be in that particular skill area.

1. *Prospecting.* On a scale of 1 to 10, how good are you at prospecting? A score of 10 would mean that you have all the prospects that you could possibly speak with, and you are booked solid with new prospects for the next two or three weeks or even for the next two or three months.

A score of 1 would mean that you have no prospects at all. You have no idea who you are going to speak with next.

This is the easiest area to score yourself. A score of 5 would mean that 50 percent of your time is already taken up with pre-arranged appointments. A score of 7 would mean that 70 percent of your time is taken up with prearranged appointments.

How would you score yourself in the area of prospecting on a scale of 1 to 10? Write in your score: _____

2. *Building Rapport and Trust.* This is an essential part of successful selling. A score of 10 means that you get along wonderfully well with almost everyone you talk to. You like them and they like you.

A score of 1 would mean that you don't particularly like yourself or your prospects. You are uncomfortable when you talk to them, and you seldom get a second chance to meet with them.

The good news in building rapport and trust is that the more you like yourself, the more you will like other people and the more they will like you. As you work on your self-confidence and self-esteem, by having clear goals and working your plans each day so that you feel happy and in control of your life, you will become a far more positive and likable person in your sales activities.

Give yourself a score of 1 to 10 in terms of how well you get along with most of your prospects in the first meeting and in subsequent meetings. Write down your score: _____

3. *Identifying Problems.* The most important part of the initial sales contact, and the ongoing sales relationship, is your ability to clearly identify exactly what it is that your prospect wants, needs, and will pay for that you can offer. You identify needs by asking carefully thought out, structured questions that elicit valuable information that enables you to tailor your product or service offering so that it genuinely helps your customers to improve their lives or work.

A score of 10 in identifying problems would mean that you have a carefully structured series of questions, from the general to the particular, that you ask each prospect. At the end of your initial conversation, both you and the prospect are crystal clear that a need or a problem exists that your product or service can satisfy or solve.

On the other hand, a score of 1 in this area would mean that your sales conversation is random and haphazard, like a drunk lurching from lamppost to lamppost, and at the end of the conversation the customer has no idea what you are talking about or why he should see you again.

In the area of identifying your customers' problems, give yourself a score of 1 to 10: _____

4. *Presenting Solutions.* This is where most sales are made. A score of 10 in presenting solutions would mean that your presentation is smooth, professional, persuasive, and, at the end, your customer is eager to enjoy the benefits of what you sell and is ready to buy.

A score of 1, on the other hand, means that your presentation is unclear and confused, and, at the end, the customer has no idea why she would want to buy from you or buy at all. Instead, the customer says, "Let me think it over."

Give yourself a score from 1 to 10: _____

5. *Answering Objections.* A score of 10 in answering objections means that you have thought through every objection that an intelligent prospect is likely to give you, and you have developed a clear and persuasive answer to each objection. Once you have answered an objection, the customer is satisfied and never brings it up again.

At the end of the scale, a score of 1 in answering objections means that each time you hear an objection, you are discouraged and disappointed. You become angry or defensive. You have no idea what to say to the customer to satisfy him that your product or service is a good choice.

Give yourself a score from 1 to 10 on answering objections: _____

6. *Closing the Sale.* To earn a 10 in this area, you would need to have a series of closing questions that you are prepared to ask at exactly the right time and in exactly the right way. You calmly and professionally wrap up the sale by getting a commitment from your customer to take action, or getting a signature on an order form or a check. You close your sales consistently and with little or no stress.

By comparison, a grade of 1 means that you do not know how to ask for the order. When the end of the presentation comes, you become nervous and panicky. You are unclear about what to do or say.

Give yourself a grade of 1 to 10 on your ability to close the sale:

_____

7. *Resales and Referrals.* To earn a 10 in this area, you have to create a "golden chain" of resales and referrals from satisfied customers. You take such good care of your customers that they want to buy from you again and tell their friends to buy from you as well.

A score of 1 would mean that, after you have made a single sale, the customer never buys from you again and never gives you any references or referrals to other potential customers.

Good salespeople structure their work with a goal of selling "by referral only." Based on the percentage of your sales that come from resales and referrals, as opposed to brand-new business, give yourself a score of 1 to 10: _____

Remember: Wherever you have given yourself a score below a 7 in any of these skill areas, it indicates that the skill area is holding you back from realizing your full potential in terms of sales and income.

Your Limiting Skill

In every sales career, the individual has a "limiting factor" to sales success. This is almost invariably your weakest area.

In which of the seven important key result areas have you given yourself the lowest score? The answer is important for you to know. You can be excellent at six out of seven of these key result areas of selling, but it is the one area where you are weak that sets the lid on how much you can sell and earn.

Here is the key question: What one skill, if you were absolutely excellent at it, consistently, would have the greatest positive impact on your sales and your income?

This is one of the most important questions you will ever ask and answer. What one skill would help you the most? Whatever it is, set it as a goal. Write it down and make a plan for its accomplishment. Work on improving yourself in that one skill area every day until you become completely confident and competent in your performance.

The key result areas (KRA) approach represents a holistic picture of the entire sales process. To identify your weakest area, write down all seven KRAs on a piece of paper. When you lose a sale, put a tally mark next to the KRA that represents at what stage you felt that the sale was lost. After a week, go back and look at your total tally marks. Where you have the most marks represents your bottleneck, your weakest key skill. Immediately go to work to alleviate this bottleneck by improving in that area. When you have upgraded yourself in this key result area, your next weakest area will emerge. Continue to track the point at which you feel you are losing the sale, and work to upgrade yourself in that area until you become fully rounded and excellent at the entire sales process.

—MT

ACTION EXERCISES

Now, here are some questions you can ask and answer to apply these ideas to your sales activities:

1. In what three ways are you in business for yourself?

2. What are three ways that you can determine your own income in sales?

3. What are the three most important activities in selling?

4. What are three of the characteristics of the top 10 percent of salespeople in your field?

5. In what three areas do you need to plan every day in advance to achieve your sales and income goals?

6. What is your weakest important skill area in selling?

7. What one skill, if you developed and did it in an excellent fashion, would have the greatest positive impact on your sales career?

Finally, what one action are you going to take immediately as a result of what you have learned in this chapter?

PROSPECTING POWER

*The quality of a person's life is in direct proportion
to their commitment to excellence, regardless of
their chosen field of endeavor.*
—Vince Lombardi

TWO OF THE MOST important requirements for success in selling, or in any other field, are focus and concentration. Focus means that you are absolutely clear about what it is you are trying to accomplish and exactly what steps you are going to have to take to realize that goal. Concentration means that you have developed the ability to concentrate single-mindedly, all day long, on doing the most important things you can do to achieve your most important sales and income goals.

The most important part of selling is prospecting, because this process fills your sales funnel in the first place. Just as the most important part of marketing is lead generation, the most vital key to sales success is finding qualified people to talk to about your product or service. The highest-paid salespeople have the best strategies and plans to develop qualified prospects, in quantity, who can and will buy from them within a reasonable period of time.

Fortunately, like all sales skills, prospecting is learnable. You can become absolutely excellent at finding new, better, higher-potential people who can lead you to lucrative sales. When you apply the best prospecting techniques to your sales work, you'll increase the number of sales you make, and it will be easier and faster than ever before.

A Fortune 500 company that I worked with had a professional approach to the sales funnel. The sales cycle—the amount of time from the first contact to the closed sale—was about seven months. From experience, the company knew the exact number of interested prospects who would eventually become customers over that seven-month period.

The salespeople were trained to fill their funnel in the first five months of the year if they wanted to make quota and achieve their income goals. Since it took seven months, on average, for a customer to move through the funnel, any customers who were not already in the funnel by the end of April would probably not buy in that calendar year. You should use the same type of thinking in your own sales work.

A basic rule of selling success is for you to never let your funnel become empty. The old sales adage, "Always be closing," has been replaced in modern selling with the rule, "Always be prospecting."

The Power of No

Perhaps the biggest single obstacle to your contacting and talking to all the prospects you need to fill your sales pipeline is the fear of rejection—also known as *call reluctance*. This is the fear of hearing the word "no" when you call on people. It is the fear of disapproval, dissatisfaction, rudeness, or negativity from other people.

When we were children, our favorite word was "yes." Can we have some candy? Yes. Can we go out to play? Yes. Can I have a toy? *Yes.* Can I stay up later? *Yes.* We loved the word "yes."

Simultaneously, we learned to hate the word "no." It always stood for denial or deprivation of some kind. Soon, we become conditioned to seek out those things that bring a "yes" and to avoid the "no." This attraction and aversion to *yes* and *no* then influences our entire lives, including our relationships with other people, especially the opposite sex, and our careers, the work we choose and the way we do it.

People seek out careers where they will be treated in a way that's consistent with their levels of self-esteem and self-confidence. Many people take back-office and low-level jobs that are safe and secure and entail no criticism or rejection of any kind. Abraham Maslow, the pioneering psychologist, once said, "The history of modern man is the story of people selling themselves short."

But the fact is that it is impossible to succeed in selling unless you are willing to hear the word "no" over and over again. The more times you hear *no*, the more you will get to *yes* as well. The more times you get rejected, the more times you will succeed. The more you get rejected, the more money you will earn, and the more successful you will be.

Imagine that your current way of thinking is like an old switchboard with cables that have to be put into different plugs. Your job is to take your plug out of the fear of rejection and transfer it to the desire for success. Instead of thinking of a "no" as a negative thing, you instead reinterpret it as a positive thing.

A friend of mine was thinking of quitting his sales job. He told his sales manager that he just could not stand the rejection. He was keeping track of his calls and found that he was being rejected nineteen times out of twenty. He had to make twenty calls to make a single sale. He was discouraged and ready to try something else.

Then his manager asked him, "How much do you earn for each sale that you make?"

He replied, "About $500."

The sales manager then asked, "If you divide twenty calls into $500, how much is that per call?

"It works out to $25 per call," he said. The sales manager then asked, smiling, "In what other line of work can you earn $25 for every phone call you make, whether they buy or not? The fact is that each person you call on is paying you, and the person who finally buys is when you collect."

My friend was transformed. He turned his thinking around completely. Instead of reluctantly making calls each day, he became a prospecting machine. As he made more and more calls, laughing every time someone rejected him, he became better and better at prospecting, and then better and better at the entire sales process. In one year, his ratio of calls to closes dropped from 20:1 to 15:1, then ten and five to one, and at the end of twelve months, he was making one sale for every three calls he made. His income increased 700 percent. A few years later he retired as a millionaire to a ranch in New Mexico, where he lives to this day.

Your job is not to endure the word "no" like a galley slave endures lashes on the back. Your job is to eagerly look forward to hearing the word "no" every single day. See how many times you can trigger the word. The more you hear it, the more sales you will make. The more sales you make, the more confident you will become, and your self-confidence and self-esteem will improve as well.

When you develop the habit of confronting your fears, over and over again, your fears eventually diminish. They become smaller and smaller, and then, like cigarette smoke, they simply drift away. You start to become absolutely fearless, and your sales begin to go straight up.

The "100 Calls" Method

There is a simple formula that you can use to eliminate the fear of rejection called the "100 calls method." Over the years, I moved from company to company, selling different products and services in different markets. At the beginning of each new sales job, I was always nervous and uneasy. My fears of rejection and call reluctance surged to the front of my mind and held me back from calling on new people.

Then I developed the 100 calls method. It changed my career. This method is simple. Wherever you are in your sales career, at whatever stage, you simply make a resolution to go out and call on 100 prospects as fast as you can. You combine this resolution with a decision not to care at all whether the people end up buying. As far as you are concerned, you don't care whether they respond in a positive or a negative manner. Your goal is simply to make 100 calls as quickly as you possibly can. If you make ten calls per day, you can accomplish this goal within two weeks. If you make twenty calls a day, you can achieve your goal of 100 calls in one five-day workweek.

Now, here's what happens. When you don't care whether or not you make a sale, most of your fear disappears. In fact, you begin to see it as a game. How many people can you get through to and talk to, and how fast can you do it? What I've found is that the very best prospecting comes when you both *care* and *don't care*. Of course you care about getting a positive result from your prospecting efforts. But if simultaneously you don't care if the person likes you or not, is willing to see you or not, or wants to buy your product or service or not, you maintain a sense of emotional detachment that allows you to remain calm and positive, no matter what anyone says.

Here is the most remarkable discovery. If you make 100 calls as fast as you can with no concern about whether or not people are interested, you will actually start to uncover good potential prospects. You will start to make appointments. You will actually start to make sales. By caring and yet not caring, you can break out of any sales slump and step on the accelerator of your sales career.

Many of my client companies have asked me how I can help their sales teams start the New Year off with a jolt, or how their salespeople can break out of a sales slump caused by a decline in the economy or a recession. I always tell them the same thing. Create a contest: Make it a game for your salespeople to go out and make 100 calls as fast as they can. Award prizes for the people who make 100 calls the fastest. Celebrate progress and celebrate success.

Over and over, individuals and organizations report back to me that this simple method has supercharged their sales, unlocked their energy, and given them a "fast start" on sales success for the year or for the quarter. Try it yourself and see.

Back to Basics

Prospecting is not only the most important part of selling, but simultaneously the most competitive and difficult, which is all the more reason that call reluctance is something you must overcome by repeatedly calling on new people until your fear largely disappears.

My son Michael came to me when he graduated college. He asked me what recommendation I would give him if he wanted to be a big success in business later in life. I told him that if he was up to it, he should get a job making cold calls, door-to-door, and stay at it until he was successful. If he could overcome his fear of cold-calling and develop the confidence that goes with sales success in such a difficult arena, he would be psychologically set up for life. He wouldn't be afraid of anything.

He took my advice. He got a job selling fiber-optic cable hookups to homes and apartments, knocking on doors from noon to 9:00 p.m., six days a week.

At first, which always happens to new cold-callers, he experienced an enormous amount of rejection. People slammed the door in his face and even swore at him. But he kept going. Eventually, he made his first sale, and then his second, third, and fourth.

With each sale, his confidence increased. He became more genial and friendly. He became more positive and enthusiastic. He recognized that this type of selling is merely a "numbers game." To get a certain number of customers to say "yes," you have to get a large number of people who say "no." And so he did.

Michael kept his promise to himself. He continued cold-call selling for exactly one year. As a result of his success, he became a supervisor, then a manager, then a regional manager. He recruited, trained, managed, and motivated other salespeople and helped them to become successful. By the end of a year, he told me, "Dad, I can do anything now because I'm not afraid to cold-call. I'm not afraid of anything."

Today, he is the senior marketing officer in charge of sales for a multimillion-dollar, high-tech company with operations in the United States and Europe. He is well paid, highly respected, runs a team of sales professionals, and still does cold-calling, just to keep his hand in.

Morning Is Best

One of the rules for success in selling is that you have to do a lot of things that you don't necessarily want to do in order to be able to do all the things that you really want to do. Prospecting is the most important part of selling. It is the kickoff in the game. It is the starting point of success and achievement. The sooner you begin, the better results you will get.

The best time to prospect is first thing in the morning. The ideal schedule is for you to spend the first one, two, or three hours of each day on the phone prospecting to get appointments with qualified customers. By starting your day off contacting ten or twenty people, you will be positive and motivated for the rest of the day.

Each morning, ask yourself, "Where is my next sale coming from?" Make sure that what you are doing at that moment is going to answer that question.

One of the breakthroughs in sales psychology was the discovery that there are two main types of salespeople: hunters and farmers. Hunters are those who confidently and aggressively go out and find new business. They are prospecting machines. They are not afraid to call on anyone. Even though they make up only 10 percent of a sales force, they open 80 percent of the new accounts, and sometimes more.

The other type of salesperson is the "farmer." This person is quite competent when it comes to following up on warm leads generated by the company and in maintaining customer relationships. This is a person who provides excellent customer service, calls back on a regular basis, builds long-term customer relationships, and generates a steady stream of resales and referrals.

When companies begin to divide up sales responsibilities into hunters and farmers, their overall sales go up and their levels of customer satisfaction increase. Hunters like to open an account and turn it over to the company to fulfill the sale and take care of the customer. Farmers like to take care of the customers, once the hunter has brought them in. Are you a hunter or a farmer? It is almost impossible to be both, and it is very difficult to be one if you are temperamentally suited to being the other. Which are you?

The More Experience, the Bigger the Customers

Sometimes salespeople become enthusiastic about their offering and conclude that there are prospects everywhere. Everyone who might need or benefit from their product or service is a potential customer, according to them. However, that's not necessarily the case.

You can only sell at your own level of knowledge and experience. What this means is that if you are a new salesperson or are selling a product or service for the first time, you will only be comfortable and effective selling to young and inexperienced customers. You will not be capable of developing high-quality relationships and selling to a senior person, an experienced customer with high-level needs for your product or service.

Companies like IBM and Xerox would train their new salespeople and then start them off selling typewriters (when those machines were still around) or basic copiers to small and medium-size business enterprises. The new salespeople would go from office to office and from store to store selling lower-priced products to smaller customers for whom the products were appropriate and affordable.

Over time, as these salespeople became more experienced and proficient, making more and better sales, they developed the competence and confidence to sell ever-larger products to larger and more sophisticated companies. After a few years, the IBM salesperson who had originally sold typewriters had graduated to selling complex and expensive computer systems. The Xerox salesperson who had been selling simple copiers would now be working with the printing departments of Fortune 1,000 corporations, selling complex, multifunction copiers and high-end reproduction equipment to serve high-level customer needs.

You have to start where you are. At the beginning of your career, your focus should be on seeing the greatest number of people and making the largest number of small sales. As you become more experienced and confident, like cream rising to the top, you will find yourself selling bigger and more expensive products and services to more experienced buyers with bigger budgets.

Characteristics of a Good Prospect

A good prospect has definite characteristics. The clearer you are about what constitutes an excellent prospect for your product or service, the easier it is for you to identify that prospect in the market and to eventually sell to that prospect.

Imagine you could run an ad for the "perfect prospect," without mentioning your product or service. What qualities, characteristics, and psychographic profile would you expect of the person who could buy from you the soonest? Here are nine characteristics:

1. *A good prospect is someone who has a problem that your product or service can solve efficiently and cost-effectively.* What problems does your product solve? Of all the problems that your product can solve, what is the most pressing, valuable, and important problem?

Once you are clear about the problem your product or service has been designed to solve, you then look around you in the marketplace and identify those customers that are most likely to have this exact problem. A question that salespeople often ask of a business-to-business (B2B) customer is, "What problems in your business keep you awake at night?"

2. *A good prospect has a need that your product or service can satisfy.* Every successful product or service has been developed to solve a problem or satisfy a need of some kind. What need would your

prospects have that would make them the ideal customers to purchase your product or service as soon as possible?

Prospects have three types of needs. In one case, the need may be obvious and clear. A company is in offices where the lease is expiring and it needs additional space to move to within the next three to six months. This type of need is apparent. The only question is how the need can be best satisfied.

In another case the need may be *unclear*, even though it obviously exists. A person may be suffering aches and pains of some kind, but does not know the cause. This person would be an ideal candidate for a doctor, who can conduct an accurate diagnosis and recommend the correct treatment.

Finally, the need may be *nonexistent*. Often in your sales work you will meet with a prospect and, after asking a few questions, realize that this prospect does not really need what you are selling. Sometimes, even when prospects are interested in your product or service, you, as an honest sales professional, can say that what they are using right now is quite appropriate for their needs at this moment.

3. *A good prospect has a goal that your product or service can help to achieve.* The primary buying motivation for all products and services is improvement. When a prospect has a specific desire to improve his life or work in some way, and your product or service can help him achieve that goal in a cost-effective way, this person can be a good prospect for you and your company.

4. *A good prospect has a pain or concern that your product or service can take away.* If you are selling personnel services or are an executive recruiter, the pain could be the absence of a skilled person in a key position to enable the business to operate more profitably. If the prospect is perfectly happy working with existing suppliers,

products, and services, and you cannot help the prospect to recognize that she could be much better off with your product or service, this person ceases to be a prospect.

5. *A good prospect has the power and authority to make the buying decision.* If your prospects recognize that they have a problem, goal, need, or pain, but they have no authority to make a buying decision, and you cannot get to the person with the authority, the sales process comes to a halt.

6. *A good prospect is someone who likes you and your company, as well as your product.* Once upon a time there were two young guys in college named Bill and Paul. They were typical "nerds" and spent all their time playing with computers and computer programming. They heard about an up-and-coming company that was looking for an operating system. They had the idea that they could develop at least the outline of an operating system, and if they could sell this system to this prospective client, they could then make it work.

They jumped on a plane, flew to the head office of the computer company, and made their presentation. As it happened, this company had just received a presentation for an operating system by another entrepreneur. This other entrepreneur was arrogant, rude, aggressive, and poorly dressed. He didn't even bathe. The executives of the computer company liked his operating system, but they definitely didn't like the developer. When the two college students made their presentation to the same executives, they said that they liked their ideas, but they preferred the other operating system. The prospective clients wanted to buy from the two young guys, but they wanted the other system.

The two college students flew to Seattle, went and found the entrepreneur who had developed the other system, arranged to buy the system from him, and then went back to the client company.

The client company installed and tested the operating system, it was successful, and a new business was born. The two college students were Bill Gates and Paul Allen, and the new business became Microsoft.

People are primarily emotional in their decision making, and almost all emotions revolve around how one person feels about another. The most important part of this story is that it was the positive personalities, the honesty and straightforwardness, and the likability of Bill Gates and Paul Allen that got them their first big break. Bill Gates is now one of the richest men in the world. The man who developed the original operating system died broke many years ago.

7. *A good prospect can become a multiple purchaser, if satisfied.* It is not a good use of your time and energy to spend a lot of effort making a single small sale. The kind of prospects you want to seek out and work hard to acquire are those people who have the capacity to buy large quantities of your product or service if they are happy with their first experience.

8. *A good prospect is a center of influence, someone who can open doors for you to other prospects.* Many sales organizations will bend over backward to acquire a respected individual or corporation as a customer. They will specially tailor their product or service, reduce their prices or offer them at no cost at all on a trial basis, and then overwhelm the customer with excellent service to ensure that this new customer is very happy with the product or service. Sometimes, a single sale to a highly respected customer can open the door to tens or even hundreds of other individuals or corporations who respect that customer. One satisfied customer who is well known and respected can create opportunities for you to sell more of your products and services at full price.

9. *A good prospect is easy to sell and service.* The very best prospect of all is a potential customer in the offices next to yours, on the same floor. At least, the customer is located nearby and is easy to get to.

The worst customer of all is the one located a great distance away from your offices and who is difficult to sell to and service. I'm always amazed when I hear about salespeople who jump on a plane to fly across the country to make a presentation when they have not yet canvassed their existing office building. Sometimes, there is an enormous amount of business within walking distance of your own offices.

Recognize Poor Prospects

Remember, how you feel about yourself and your work largely determines your levels of optimism, enthusiasm, and cheerfulness. When you feel positive and happy about your product or service and your work, you are much more positive and persuasive in your interactions with prospective customers.

More than anything else, continued exposure to negative people can bring you down emotionally. One negative, critical prospect or customer can deflate you for an entire day, or even a week, draining away all the energy you need to call on new customers.

This is an important point. One of your main goals as a top salesperson is to maintain high levels of positive energy. To do that, you must reduce the amount of time that you spend face-to-face with negative people. Negative people come in the form of poor prospects for what you are selling.

As soon as you recognize that you are in the presence of a negative person and poor prospect, you should move quickly to cut off the meeting, wish the person well, and get out of there. Get on to the next person, who might be far more positive and receptive to what you are offering. There is a simple rule in prospecting that says: "Some will. Some won't. So what? Someone else is waiting."

Your job is to quickly whisk through the poor prospects so that you can get to the better prospects. Resolve to spend as little time as possible with people who drag you down by recognizing the signs of a poor prospect:

▪ *A poor prospect has a difficult personality.* These people complain and criticize you, your products and services, your company, and often their own company and the people they work with. Whenever you meet a person like this, always remember that "you are not the target." This person was negative and unhappy before you got there and will continue to be negative and unhappy after you leave. A negative attitude and personality has nothing to do with your product or service. It is simply a part of the person's worldview.

When you run into a negative or unhappy person—someone who is critical and complaining—you should be exactly the opposite. Deliberately overextend yourself to be polite, gracious, and courteous. Say "please" and "thank you." When you see that you are dealing with a negative person, you stand up and say something such as, "This is perhaps not a good time to talk about my product. Why don't we get back together at a later time, when we can discuss it in greater detail?" Then you thank the person for his time and for seeing you, wish him a good day, and you depart. Your goal is to reduce the number of minutes that you spend exposed to difficult people. You will always feel happier and more buoyant when you walk away.

▪ *A poor prospect sees little benefit in what you are offering.* While a good prospect is interested in what you have to say, asks questions, and becomes involved in the conversation, a poor prospect sits there with little emotion, often regarding you suspiciously.

Again, remember that this response has nothing to do with you or your product or service offering. Many people look upon a new product or service offering as an inconvenience, an unnecessary disruption to their current lives, and a threat to their comfort zones. Think of sales as a game of Ping-Pong. You hit the ball with something that you say, and the other person hits it back. As long as the ball keeps going back and forth, you have a good sales conversation. But if the other person is uncooperative or unresponsive, the game stops.

When you seem to be getting no positive feedback or interest from the prospect, fold your cards. Cut your losses. Simply accept that this is not a good use of your time, and that somewhere, someone else who can buy your product or service is waiting. The more time you spend with this negative person, the longer you are keeping other good prospects waiting, wherever they are.

A poor prospect argues or complains continually about your price or quality. These are some of the most irritating prospects of all. They tell you that your prices are too high, that your competitor's prices and quality are better, and that your product or service is not very good. This assessment may not be true. It could be that this prospect had a bad day and you are the victim of a "drive-by shooting." The prospect unloads on you to deal with some other negative event in his life. Since you are a polite and patient sales professional, you will endure the prospect's negative assessment of your product or prices, but only for a little while.

Always be gracious. Never respond to a complaint or criticism with an answer. Instead, ask questions such as, "Why do you say that? What do you mean, exactly? Where did you get that idea (or perception)?"

By asking questions, you remain calm and positive and keep complete control over the conversation. By asking questions, you remain positive and courteous. By asking questions, you defuse any negative emotions that you might have, stemming from the negativity of the prospect.

▪ *A poor prospect is happy with his existing supplier.* If the customer is perfectly happy with the company that is currently supplying him with the same product or service that you are offering, you should just accept it and move on.

This is the kind of sales relationship that you want to develop and maintain. In this situation, take the opportunity to learn something that can help you in the future. You could ask, "What do you like most about your existing supplier?" Sometimes, a happy customer will give you valuable insights into what you need to do more of, or less of, to build and maintain high-quality customer relationships.

▪ *A poor prospect would be a small purchaser of your product or service.* Of course, there is nothing wrong with a small customer. But it is not a good idea to invest an enormous amount of time to acquire small customers, even those who are convinced that your product or service is ideal for them, when other, larger prospective customers are waiting for you to call on them.

▪ *A poor prospect is not a good source of referrals.* Many prospects (individuals and companies) are largely unknown to anyone else in your potential customer community. Even if they love your product or service, they cannot help you to get any more customers, and getting referrals should be something that is always in the back of your mind.

▪ *A poor prospect is difficult to visit or service geographically.* Remember, traveling time is "downtime." If your prospective customers are a great distance away from your office, that automatically renders them less attractive than prospects that are located much closer to you.

Guinness World Records once rated Ben Feldman the "number one salesman in the world." He is still a legend in life insurance sales. He broke every record ever set. At the peak of his career, he was earning $13 million a year in straight commission income, primarily from cold calls and the referrals that came from his sales.

Feldman is also famous for his "geographical strategy." He wanted to have dinner with his family every night in his hometown of East Liverpool, Ohio. He therefore drew a fifty-mile circle around his home and disciplined himself to work within that circle for most of his career, so he would always be able to make it home for dinner after his last call. When he began his insurance sales career in 1942, East Liverpool's population was 20,000. Fifty years later, when Feldman was the highest-paid salesman in the world, East Liverpool still had a population of 20,000. By hunting and farming in that small area, Feldman was able to set sales records that have yet to be broken.

Strategic Thinking

There are four key strategic thinking principles that you can use to improve your prospecting results: specialization, differentiation, segmentation, and concentration. By looking at your products and your customers through the lens of these four principles, you will be able to better decide who you are going to call on before you begin work.

1. *Specialization.* Each product or service can do some things and cannot do others. Clarity is essential. What exactly is your product or service designed to do? What result does it achieve? What problem does it solve? What goal does it help a customer to achieve? What pain does it take away?

In clearly identifying your area of specialization, use the PTBS—problem to be solved—approach. Keep asking, "What is the problem that my product or service is designed to solve?" Then look at the total market and ask, "Who are the prospects who have or are experiencing this problem the most intensely?"

2. *Differentiation.* All successful selling involves differentiating your product or service (and yourself) from that of your competitors, or from whatever it is that your prospective customer is currently using. Differentiation refers to your *competitive advantage.* Every product must have a competitive advantage that makes it a superior choice in comparison with its competitors in achieving the same goal or solving the same problem.

What is your area of excellence? Most important, in differentiation you must identify your USP—unique selling proposition. To be successful, every product or service must have something unique that sets it apart and above all other competitors in its market. Sometimes this USP is clear and obvious. Sometimes it is unclear and must be discovered and emphasized. In markets with many products and services, there is no USP or competitive advantage. In this case, an offering can only be sold by lowering the price.

Imagine someone asking you, "Tell me the one unique benefit that your product or service offers me that I cannot get anywhere else. Tell me the specific reason that I should buy it from you rather than your competitor." How would you answer?

Jack Welch, when he was CEO of General Electric, said, "If you don't have competitive advantage, don't compete." Peter Drucker said that if you don't have a competitive advantage, you must immediately go to work to develop one, or to recognize a point of differentiation that already exists that you may not be using in your current marketing and sales.

3. *Segmentation.* Once you have determined your area of specialization and your unique selling proposition, you now identify the specific customer segment in your marketplace that can most benefit from your product or service offering, and can buy it and pay for it the most rapidly.

4. *Concentration.* This is where you focus all your energies on your very best prospects, the ones most likely to buy the soonest. Focus all your advertising, promotion, and sales activities on contacting exactly those customers who want, need, can use, and can afford your product or service.

Customer Analysis

Analyzing your current prospects and customers is something you do before you begin your prospecting activities. By looking at who is buying your product or service today, and who is most interested in it, you can identify the very best places to focus and concentrate your energies to make the most sales in the shortest period of time.

Here are twelve questions to ask and answer:

1. Who is using your product or service today?

2. Who will be using it in the future, based on current trends?

3. Why should somebody buy your product at all?

4. If someone should buy your product, why should they buy it from your company rather than from some other company?

5. If customers have decided to buy from your company, why should they buy the product or service from you *personally*, rather than from someone else in your company?

6. Who exactly is your customer? Who buys from you most readily? There are always some people who are easier and faster sells for you than others.

7. Why does your customer buy your product or service? What specific benefits does the customer receive from your product or service?

8. Who or what is your *competition* for the customer? Your competition is any alternative product or service in the market, or any alternate use of the same amount of money that the customer would spend on what you're selling. When I worked with the cruise line industry, the competition was not other cruise lines. The competition was "land-based vacations." For cruise operators, the goal was not to position themselves against other cruise ships, but to position themselves against vacations at the beach or in the mountains.

9. Why do customers buy from your competition? Specifically? Do you know?

10. What advantages do customers perceive in buying from your competitor that they do not perceive when considering buying from you?

11. What *weaknesses* do customers perceive in your product or service offering? This is a good question to ask when you are dealing with a reluctant prospect. You can say, "No product or service is perfect, including this one. What weaknesses do you see in this product (or service) that I have just shown you?" When you ask this question, you will be amazed at how open your prospects will be in pointing out to you the product or service weaknesses, and how very often you can find a way to resolve the concerns expressed.

12. How can you offset these perceived weaknesses? Sometimes, you can point out that the weaknesses in your product or service, in comparison with your competitors, are not really that important in making this buying decision. You can point out that the strong points

that you offer are vastly more important to customer satisfaction than the small areas where you may not be as strong as others.

Who Are Your Noncustomers?

People who do not buy product, either from you or from your competitors, are called "noncustomers." Sometimes by identifying your noncustomers, and finding out what it is in their perceptions that stops them from buying at all, you can create an entirely new market in which there is little or no competition.

Why don't these people buy, from you or from anyone else? Why are they noncustomers? What is it that they see or don't see in using or not using your product or service? How can you change their perceptions so that they see what you are selling as being both desirable and necessary?

Henry Ford's first automobile was very expensive relative to the income earned by the average person or family. Nonetheless, in a field that was eventually filled with dozens of automobile manufacturers, he was able to take 26 percent of the market for the "horseless carriage."

Then he had an insight. If he could mass-produce his automobiles and bring down the price, average people could afford to buy a car. If average people were able to buy a car, including the people who worked in his factories, he could dramatically increase the size of his market and the volume of his sales.

Five years later, Ford's market share had grown from 26 percent to 62 percent, making him the most successful industrialist and the richest man in the world. He succeeded by identifying his noncustomers and providing them with a product that vastly improved the quality of their lives. Is this somehow possible for you?

Selling to Your Ideal Customer

Who is your ideal customer? If you could put an ad in the paper for "ideal customers," just as if you were placing an ad to hire a new person for your company, how would you describe this customer, in every detail? Especially, how would you describe your perfect customer if you could not mention your company, your product, or your service?

Begin with the customer's *demographics*. What is the age, education level, income, occupation, location, family situation, and current life situation of your ideal customer? Where is your ideal customer located—geographically and socially or economically? Your ideal customer may be someone who works within driving distance of your office (recall Ben Feldman's famous geographic strategy). Sometimes your ideal customer is someone who works at a particular job, at a particular level, in a particular type of industry.

Identify the *psychographics* of your customer, which are increasingly more important than anything else. What is it that your ideal customer wants, desires, and hopes for in life that your product or service can help him achieve in some way? What are the worries, fears, and problems that keep your ideal customer up at night? What are the customer's aspirations for the future?

Once you have a list of the qualities, both demographic and psychographic, of your ideal customer, review the list and select the top three to five qualities or characteristics of the person who could and would most readily buy your product or service.

One of my clients is a large national company that set up a sales office in San Diego a few years ago. The company sold large business systems to large companies. The company's salespeople identified the six largest companies in the San Diego area. They then worked out a complete strategy to penetrate each of those companies.

The most important decision maker in each of the six target companies was the senior purchasing manager. This was the key executive who evaluated the purchases of the systems they were selling and who made the final decision. For five years, they worked to penetrate each of these six companies, meeting and talking with lower-level people in procurement and purchasing and gradually working up to the point of playing golf and going out for dinner with the key decision makers in each company. At the end of five years, exactly on schedule, every one of those major companies was using their business services exclusively.

In B2B sales, the primary buying motivation is to make or save money, or to gain or save time, and preferably both. The most important concern is what is called "time-to-payback." The attractiveness of a product or service, and the speed at which a company will buy that product or service, is largely determined by how quickly the company thinks that product or service will pay for itself. In effect, if you are selling a product or service to a qualified corporate prospect, your product or service will actually turn out to be "free" because the customer will benefit financially in a way that more than pays for the cost of the product or service. Once the product has paid for itself, it yields an ongoing stream of financial benefits.

When I explain this concept to the senior executives of Fortune 1,000 companies, I tell them that their entire marketing and sales effort must be focused on demonstrating that what they offer is "free, plus a profit." At first, they are surprised at this kind of positioning. But they quickly come to understand its importance to qualified prospects. A qualified prospect is someone who can genuinely benefit well in excess of the cost of the product or service, whatever it is. In effect, if a prospect buys the product or service, it will turn out to be free over time, and often quite quickly.

You should think about those prospects in your marketplace for whom your product or service can be "free, plus a profit." These will be the easiest people to talk to and to sell to, and the people who will be most appreciative of your product or service offering.

Convincing the Prospect to Buy

Once you are clear about the identity of your ideal customer, the next question to address is, How can you best convince your ideal prospect to buy? What are the key arguments you can use, in order of priority? For you to win the sale, what must the customer be convinced of?

In Chapter 2, we said that the most important and highly paid skill you have is your ability to think. The more time you take to think through exactly who your prospects are, why they would buy, and the unique benefits that your product or service can offer them, the easier it is for you to identify exactly those prospects in the marketplace who will be the happiest to speak with you.

Your job is to keep your sales pipeline full. The more and better prospects you are working with at any given time, the more likely it is that you'll have the kind of sales you need to be among the top people in your field. You must always be thinking about better ways to get better prospects. Think through who they are, where they are, and why they might buy from you.

In prospecting, activity is essential, but pushing yourself or your reps too hard can be costly. If salespeople push too hard for too long, they can burn out. I've seen this happen with several salespeople I have trained and managed, and it has happened to me personally.

In my first sales position, I was driving an hour to work, knocking on fifty doors a day, conducting at least one sales training meeting, personally training new recruits, driving my sales reps to their areas, supervising them to make sure they were being productive, conducting an end-of-day review meeting, reporting results to my superiors, driving one hour back home, and then doing it all again, six days a week.

When you work at that pace, you make compromises in your diet, exercise, and how much time you spend with your family. You start to wear out and stop becoming effective in selling. The harder you work, the fewer sales you make. On the other hand, the best and most lucrative sales I have made have been from a relaxed, healthy state of mind and body, not a frantic and exhausted one.

To maintain a high level of successful prospecting activity, the most important lesson you can learn is to bite off what you can chew comfortably every day, and do only that. It is much better to make forty calls every day for a year than to make a hundred calls a day for a month. The best and most productive sales professionals do daily what most sales professionals do occasionally. In setting your daily goals, set them so that you can maintain that pace indefinitely.

—MT

ACTION EXERCISES

Now, here are some exercises, including questions to ask and answer, for applying these ideas to your sales activities.

1. What are the three main benefits to you for becoming excellent at prospecting?

2. List three characteristics of an excellent prospect for what you sell.

3. List three characteristics of a poor prospect for your product or service.

4. What exactly is your product or service designed to do to improve the life or work of your customer?

5. What are your three unique selling features or competitive advantages?

6. What specific customers in the marketplace can best benefit from the special qualities or benefits of your product or service?

7. List three reasons a potential customer should buy from you and your company rather than from your best competitor.

Finally, what one action are you going to take immediately as a result of what you have learned in this chapter?

RELATIONSHIP SELLING

*Always bear in mind that your own resolution to
succeed is more important than any other factor.*
—Abraham Lincoln

ONE OF THE GREAT breakthroughs in modern selling is the discovery of the concept of "positioning"—how the customer thinks and feels about you. It is the sum total result of all your interactions with the customer and is greatly influenced by the first impression. Your positioning in the customer's mind and heart is perhaps the most powerful factor in determining how much you sell and how quickly you sell it.

If you like, respect, and care about the person selling a product, and you have complete confidence that the product is of excellent quality and will help you immediately to improve your life in some way, you are 95 percent of the way to a buying decision before the salesperson even opens his mouth.

Positioning is everything. How are you and your company, product, or service thought about by the customer? What are the words that the customer uses when he thinks about you or describes you to others?

Imagine that one of your customers called you up and told you that she was about to have lunch with one of your prospective customers. This customer likes you and wants to help you. She asks, "Exactly what would you like me to tell this prospective customer about you? What words would you like me to use to describe you that would be most helpful to your getting the sale?"

How would you answer? This is such an important question that it cannot be left to chance. And as it happens, there is a "single attribute theory" of positioning. The idea is that you may leave a lot of impressions in the customer's mind, but one attribute will predominate. This attribute is the trigger that determines whether the prospect buys from you, buys again, or tells her friends.

Imagine that the brain is like a warehouse full of filing cabinets. Each customer has a mental file for storing every impression and experience regarding you and your company, from the very first contact. You also have a mental file on every person, place, and situation in your life, going back to early childhood. Some of these mental files are thin, perhaps a memory of a restaurant where you had dinner in a foreign city one time many years ago. Some of these files are thick, like the file that you have for your spouse, your children, your parents, your friends, your education, and your career. But each time you have a new experience, you immediately open up a mental file and put the first impression in that file. And this first impression is often lasting, sometimes for the rest of your life.

Your position in your customers' mind—the way they think and feel about you—determines if they buy, how quickly they buy, how much they negotiate, and whether they buy again or recommend you to their friends.

The Golden Triangle of Selling

This formula is based on the experience of top salespeople everywhere. Thousands of customers have been interviewed over the years and asked specifically what they thought about the best salespeople who called on them. They consistently described top salespeople, in every industry, worldwide, in three main ways—as friend, adviser, and teacher.

1. *Friend.* Customers viewed the salesperson as a friend who genuinely cared about their well-being, even more than making a sale. When your customers begin to think of you as a personal friend who just happens to be in the business of selling a product or service that they purchase, they will remain loyal to you for as long as you represent that product or service. It will be almost impossible for a competitor to get to that customer with a better price or offer. As Shakespeare wrote, those friends you have, once tried, bind them to you with "hoops of steel." When you develop a genuine friendship with a customer, you create unbreakable bonds of loyalty that keep that customer coming back to you for your products and services year after year. (We'll come back to the subject of friendship later in this chapter.)

2. *Adviser.* Customers thought the best salesperson was a trusted expert who gave good advice to help them improve their lives or work, both with the product or service the salesperson was selling and in other areas as well. When customers begin to see you as an adviser, as the go-to person in your field, they eventually reach the point where they will not buy from anyone else but you.

How can you tell if your customers see you as an adviser? Simple. When they are approached by a competitor with a product or service that's similar to what you sell, they will phone you personally and ask for your advice on the competitor's product. They know that you will always tell the truth and will guide them to make the right decision. When your customers start calling you and asking for your advice about your competitors, you know that you are rising into the top 10 percent of sales professionals, in terms of both sales results and income.

3. *Teacher.* Customers saw top salespeople as teachers who showed them how to best benefit from the product or service they were selling. More than this, the best salespeople took the trouble to educate customers on background and side issues pertinent to making the best choices. This is an important discovery in modern selling that will have an effect on your results for the rest of your career. The following story reveals the importance of teaching in selling.

The IBM Story

In the 1980s, IBM was one of the most admired companies in the world. Then, a new president was appointed with a new philosophy. He concluded that IBM no longer needed to spend so much time and effort in the process of selling its products and services. The company was now far beyond the "grubby" business of sales and marketing. Instead, IBM was an "engineering" company.

With this new approach, the salespeople were treated as if they belonged to the sleazy side of the business. They were saddled with enormous paperwork requirements that they had to complete after every customer contact. The sales managers were required to spend virtually all their time reviewing the reports from the salespeople. As a result, the salespeople spent less and less time in the field. If customers had questions, they were told to call an 800 number, where they could be serviced by a faceless technician.

IBM's competitors saw, for the first time, a tremendous opportunity. They began to offer extensive in-service training and workshops to guide their customers to get the very best results possible out of the equipment and software they were selling.

IBM sales plummeted. The share price dropped. The experts on Wall Street started speculating about the need to break IBM up into four divisions and perhaps sell them off to competitors. The company virtually fell out of the sky.

The board of directors finally took action. They fired the president and eventually all the executives that he had put into place. They did an extensive search before finally hiring Lou Gerstner, who was CEO of Nabisco, to turn the company around if he could.

Gerstner had originally worked for McKinsey & Company, one of the best management consulting firms in the world. He called them and asked for their help and guidance. McKinsey & Company sent in a team of specialists, who fanned out around the country to interview customers and competitors in order to find out what had happened to cause IBM to get into so much trouble so quickly.

What they found was that, in its peak years, IBM salespeople spent a lot of time working hand in hand, shoulder to shoulder, with their customers to help them to maximize their investment in IBM products. But under the new (and now past) president, they were almost forbidden to spend time with customers. As a result, the customers became easy pickings for competitors.

With these insights, Gerstner did two things. First of all, he significantly increased the size of the sales force. He took back-office people and engineers, trained them in sales, and sent them out to call on customers. Second, he mandated that from now on,

75 percent of the time of individual salespeople and sales managers would be spent in the field, working with customers, rather than in the office. If there were call reports to be filled out, sales assistants were hired to take care of the paperwork.

In no time at all, the company turned completely around. It went from massive losses to massive profits. The share price went up more than 50 percent. IBM once again became one of the most admired and most profitable companies in the world. It was a close shave.

The lesson from the IBM story is that you and your salespeople should not underestimate the importance of teaching your customers how to maximize their investment in whatever it is you are selling. It is not fair, nor is it right, for you to drop off a product or service once sold and just assume that the customer is going to figure out how to get the most out of it.

Three Selling Strategies

The Golden Triangle of Selling—being a friend, an adviser, and a teacher—requires that you use these three strategies simultaneously in your selling work. When you become fluent in each of these strategies, your sales results will soar. Your customers will be happy. They will buy more from you, and you will earn more than ever before.

RELATIONSHIP SELLING

This is where you position yourself as a friend. You take the time to build a relationship first. You ask a lot of questions and listen closely to the answers. You take an interest in the total customer, including not only the parts of his work or life that determine whether he buys from you, but also his likes and dislikes, his current position and past history, and other things about his life that are usually more important than whatever it is you are selling.

But there is a danger in relationship selling that you must avoid. It is that, in becoming so concerned about the quality of your relationship, you become hypersensitive to the customer's thoughts and feelings. You want the customer to like you so much that you avoid asking the customer to buy your product, and you bend over backward to satisfy every desire of the customer, even if the requests are unreasonable or unaffordable. It is true that the relationship comes first in every sales transaction, because it is only in establishing a good relationship that you will be able to proceed in the sales process. The relationship is important, but it is not everything.

Relationship selling will be the primary topic of the rest of this chapter.

CONSULTATIVE SELLING

You position yourself with customers as a consultant, expert, and trusted adviser by focusing on helping them to solve their problems or achieve their goals. Customers are busy. The very best customers are overwhelmed with too much to do and too little time. If they are going to carve out a piece of their day to spend time with you, they must feel that it is a valuable and worthwhile investment.

When you position yourself as a consultant, you ask well-thought-out and penetrating questions of customers that help them to think better and more clearly about their situations, their futures, and their real needs and requirements. By asking intelligent questions of your customers, you make yourself valuable to them and cause them to be open if not eager to seeing you again and again.

The relationship side of the sale, the *emotional* part, is important. But the real "beef" of the sales relationship is when your customers see you as important and essential to improving their lives or work in a cost-effective way. The more you ask good questions designed to uncover the customer's problems or needs and give good advice to solve those problems and achieve the customer's goals, the more the customer sees you as a valuable resource.

We will cover consultative selling in depth in Chapter 5.

EDUCATIONAL SELLING

This is where you position yourself as a teacher, showing prospects how they can best benefit from using your product or service. The interesting thing about teaching, especially during the presentation part of professional selling, is that every "lesson" that you give increases the customers' buying desire and increases their loyalty to you and your product after the purchase.

Not only that, the better that you "school" your customers, the more capable they are of telling other people about what you sell and how they can best benefit. By taking the time to teach, you can actually turn your customers into advocates who end up selling your product to other people by talking about the benefits that they are enjoying.

The Emotional Foundation of Relationships

Selling has changed considerably in the last few years—from a rapid, impersonal process to a slower, more people-intensive process. The heart of the sale today is contained in the quality of relationships that you form with your prospects and your customers. The very best and most successful salespeople are those who are most capable of entering into and maintaining the highest-quality relationships with people who can buy from them and recommend them to their friends and associates.

The same qualities and behaviors that enable you to get along well with the most important people in your personal life are the same behaviors that enable you to develop long-term, high-trust relationships with customers.

According to Theodore Levitt, longtime professor at the Harvard Business School, all sales in the twenty-first century will be relationship sales. They will largely be based on how the customer feels about the salesperson and the company offering the products and services.

People do business with people they like. They refuse to do business with people they don't like, even if they want or prefer the product or service that the unlikable person is offering. If the relationship is right, the details will not get in the way of the sale. But if the relationship is not right, the details will trip you up every step of the way.

Sometimes I will ask sales audiences, "How much of a person's thinking is logical/rational and how much is emotional?" They will answer, "80/20! 90/10! 50/50!" and so on.

That's when I stop and point out that, like them, customers are 100 percent emotional. People make decisions emotionally and then justify them logically. People are completely dominated by their feelings, whether or not they mask them, suppress them, or ignore them.

The basic rule is that "emotions distort valuations." What I mean is that any emotion, positive or negative, exaggerates and intensifies the actions and reactions of the person involved. If I like you, I view everything you say and offer in a more favorable light. If I am neutral toward you, or even worse, if I don't particularly like you, I will see everything that you say and offer in a negative light.

The Friendship Factor

The key to success in sales is to develop an ever-widening circle of professional and commercial friendships. The three keys to developing the friendship factor are caring, consideration, and courtesy.

First, you make it clear that you *care* about the customer by asking good questions and paying close attention to everything the customer says. You have heard it said that "they don't care how much you know until they know how much you care." The very first unspoken question that prospects are going to have when they you meet you for the first time is, "Do you care about me?"

You express *consideration* for the customer beyond the product or service offering by asking questions and taking an interest in the customer's life and work apart from the product you are discussing. Even though this seems to be a roundabout way of developing a sales relationship, it is usually the fastest and most direct way. By taking an interest in the customer, you cause the customer to naturally be more interested in you and to like you more.

The third part of the friendship factor is *courtesy*. The very fact that you are polite, gracious, and courteous with everyone you meet in the customer's home or office, and especially with the customer himself, sets you apart from people who are focused on the sale to the exclusion of everything else.

One of the best ways to open your first meeting with the client is to say something like, "Thank you very much for your time. I know how busy you are." This simple statement positions you as a professional. You are acknowledging that the person you are talking to is important and has done you a favor by giving you time. This simple statement usually melts the ice and causes the prospect to be more open to what you have to say. It starts the sales relationship off on the right foot.

The highest-paid salespeople look upon each new customer interaction as the beginning of a long-term friendship. It is not unusual for a first contact in business to turn into a friendship that lasts many years, both professionally and privately. In my own career, I have formed business friendships that have continued for more than thirty years. And these friendships have resulted in enormous amounts of sales and business.

The Power of Reputation

The fastest-growing and most profitable companies also have the very best reputations in the marketplace for their products and services. For example, Nordstrom has cultivated a national reputation for excellent customer service. With hundreds of competing stores in every market where Nordstrom opens a store, the retailer soon dominates virtually all other competitors with the quality of its customer service. This is no accident. Nordstrom's reputation is extremely important and is cultivated in every customer interaction.

A large part of Google's success lies in the incredibly talented people that it attracts to work for the company. Google consistently leads among companies rated to be "a great place to work." It does everything possible to make the experience of working at Google a positive and enriching experience. As a result, the smartest and most talented high-tech experts and entrepreneurs line up to apply for jobs at Google whenever there is an opening.

What is your company's reputation? How is your company thought about, talked about, and described to others? What words do people use when they describe your company to a noncustomer? Your answers to these questions largely determine the future and fate of your business.

In the 1800s, and in the early twentieth century, there was a coffee grower and exporter in the Hawaiian Islands called Lion Coffee. Its reputation for quality products, service, delivery, and efficiency was excellent. Over the decades, the founders died off, the company changed hands several times, and it was finally shut down. Then a group of businesspeople decided to start a company growing, roasting, packaging, and distributing coffee in the Hawaiian Islands. In their due diligence, they came across the records and history of "Lion Coffee."

They quickly discovered that the name was still remembered and almost legendary for the quality of its products. They paid the heirs and descendants of Lion Coffee several million dollars just to buy the *name* for their new business. Even though the company had not been active for many years, the name was still so powerful that when they relaunched the company under the new brand, the positive associations with the company persisted and, within a few years, it was the most respected and most successful company on the Hawaiian Islands, and still is today.

Your Personal Reputation

By the same token, your reputation is your most valuable asset in life and in business. It is the qualities and behaviors that you are known by and remembered for. It is how people think about you and talk about you. As Shakespeare observed, he who steals my purse steals trash, but he who steals my good name, steals all.

In business, your reputation, or how you are known to your customers, is the single most important determinant of your level of sales and your income. And the great rule with regard to reputation is that "everything counts"!

Everything you do, or neglect to do, *counts*. Everything you say counts. Everything helps or hurts. Everything adds up or takes away. A reputation takes a long time to build; it requires tremendous integrity and work to maintain your reputation, but it can be quickly lost by making a single mistake.

Dan Sullivan, a business coach, says that there are three keys to building a quality reputation in sales: (1) Say please and thank you. (2) Show up on time; always be punctual. (3) Fulfill your promises; always do what you say you will do. They sound quite simple, but it is amazing how many sales professionals forget to be polite, arrive late for sales appointments, and neglect to follow through with what they promised they would do during the call.

The Reputations of Top Salespeople

Your positioning in the minds and hearts of your customers, how they think about you and talk about you when you are not there, is the summary statement of your reputation. All top salespeople are described in positive if not enthusiastic terms by their customers. And it seems that customers use the same words to describe the top salespeople in every industry.

First, they say, "He works for me." What this means is that the salesperson takes such a close interest in his customers' situations and needs that customers actually feel as if the salesperson is more concerned about them than about making a sale. This is one of the most important perceptions that you can develop, and you develop it by focusing on customer needs at all times, with your product or service always coming in second or third. Customers will sometimes describe the salesperson as "an unpaid member of my own staff." In this sense, customers are saying that they can call on the salesperson at any time, by phone or by e-mail, when they have a problem or need that involves the product or service offering.

Another way that customers describe top salespeople is "as a consultant, a friend, a trusted adviser." The way that the salesperson builds the *perception* of being a trusted adviser in the mind of the prospect is by asking questions and seeking ways to help the prospect achieve his goals and improve his life or business. The more you focus on helping your prospect, the more the prospect will view you as someone who is different and more helpful than your competitors.

Sometimes customers will say that the salesperson "really understands my situation." How does the customer form that perception about you? Simple. You continually ask questions about the customer's situation, listen attentively to the answers, and offer ideas and assistance to help the customer in that area.

Customers, like everyone else, are lazy. They seek out the path of least resistance to get the things they want, the fastest and easiest way possible. Once customers have formed a relationship with you, and are convinced that you know and understand them and their situations, they will be reluctant to start all over again with a new representative of a new company to form a new relationship.

People very quickly fall into a "comfort zone." They become comfortable doing things a certain way and are reluctant to change or to try something new. For this reason, when you build and maintain a high-quality relationship with your customers, they will often stay with you and continue to buy from you for an indefinite period of time.

A Fatal Decision

One of my clients is a manufacturing company in the Chicago area that sells machine tools to other manufacturers throughout the Midwest. One day, the company executives sat down and analyzed their sales for the year. They were surprised to find that one salesman accounted for 50 percent of their annual sales, amounting to many millions of dollars.

This salesman had been working for this company for twenty years. He had carefully cultivated his client base and built up a large "book of business." His customers bought expensive machinery from him year after year, even going into the second generation of company ownership.

My clients then made a terrible mistake. They decided that this salesman accounted for too much of their business, and, besides, he was earning far too much money. They agreed among themselves that these customers belonged to them, not the salesperson, and the salesperson should not be paid so much to service these accounts.

They called the salesman in and announced their decision to cut his territory in half and reduce his commissions. They explained to him that they felt he was being paid far too much to service their longtime customers.

The salesman was very pleasant. He pointed out that these customers were his close friends and that if the company took them away from him, and cut his income, he would have no choice but to go to a competitor and take his customers with him. He didn't want to take this step, but he would have no choice if the company insisted on its course of action.

Sadly, the executives in this company had never been salespeople. They were second-generation owners of the company and had never been in the field. They assumed, as many people without sales experience do, that sales just fall from the sky, like rain, and that all a salesperson has to do is hold out a bucket, bring in customers (and revenue), and get a commission.

The company owners proceeded with their decision. They cut his territory and his commissions. Thirty days later he submitted his resignation and went to work for a competitor that had been courting him for many years. Within twelve months, 90 percent of his customers had moved their business to his new company. The company that had dismissed the salesperson as being of only secondary importance to sales almost went bankrupt. It took them years to recover. They simply had no understanding of the importance of relationships between salespeople and customers in the highly competitive markets where product and service offerings are often similar and interchangeable.

When Relationships Are Even More Important

Relationships are even more important in certain situations or with certain types of sales. For example, the larger and more complex the sale, the more important the relationship is. In a large, complex sale, there are far too many details for the customer to analyze or comprehend. The customer must therefore make a decision based on something other than the complex details of the product or service offering alone, and that "something else" is how the customer feels about the sales representative.

The more people who will be affected by the purchase, the more important the relationship is. Customers, like everyone else, are hypersensitive to the feelings and reactions of the people with whom they work. When a decision maker considers purchasing a product or service that other people will have to implement or use, his confidence in the person selling and ultimately servicing the product is a vital factor in making the decision in the first place.

The longer the life of the product, or the longer the length of the decision to buy, the more important the relationship becomes. In fact, the relationship is paramount when a customer buys a product or service and then must use that product or service for years to get full value out of it.

IBM became one of the most respected companies in the world because it had an international reputation for taking wonderful care of its customers. Once you bought an IBM product, you never had to worry about breakdowns or malfunctions. IBM would take care of you under any circumstances, and usually quickly and efficiently.

For a first-time buyer of your product or service, the relationship is very important. In any new purchase, the prospect will be unsure about whether to proceed. The more confidence new customers have in the salesperson, and the more they trust the salesperson, then the more relaxed they will be about entering into the sales agreement in the first place.

Relationships Lower Risk

A key variable in modern selling is *risk*, or the perception of risk. A good relationship lowers the perception of risk. People will pay a lot to lower the probability of risk in any purchase decision.

When presented with a lower-priced product that has a higher risk factor, and compared with a higher-priced product with a lower risk factor, the customer will always settle the tension or stress of the buying decision by moving upward to higher price and lower risk.

Once you are clear that a prospect wants and needs what you are selling, then you must address the many concerns that will be running through the customer's mind: Will it work? Is this a good decision? Will I lose my money? Will I end up paying too much? Will I find the product cheaper somewhere else? If I buy this product or service from this company, will the seller follow through on its commitments and guarantees?

Your main job in the conversation is to clearly demonstrate to your customer, through testimonials, stories, and anecdotes, that there is virtually no risk in buying your product or service.

If your customer says, "I can get it cheaper from your competitor," you simply say, "Yes, of course. But only if you are willing to take that much of a risk." Whenever you can imply or demonstrate that buying a rival product is a riskier decision than buying from you, you increase the perceived value of your product and lower the perception of risk.

The New Model of Selling

It seems that the most successful salespeople in every industry, no matter how they have been trained, gradually migrate to using what I call "the new model of selling."

The new model of selling can be represented as an upside-down triangle with the base at the top and the apex at the bottom. This triangle is then divided into four parts. The top layer of the new model of selling, which represents 40 percent of the triangle, is *building trust*. Trust is the glue that holds relationships together. Trust is the lubricant between people that allows them to be confident in each other's company. Trust is the cement that holds together the bricks of any relationship.

When you think over your life, you will find that the most important people in your life are also the people you trust the most. Without trust, no sales relationship is possible. This is why trust is 40 percent of the relationship model.

The second part of the new model of selling, accounting for 30 percent, is *identifying needs accurately*. The more you demonstrate your desire to understand the customer's needs, the more the customer trusts and believes you. The more you ask questions and listen to the answers, the more the customer will open up to you and give you more information to help you to make a good purchase recommendation.

Here's a rule: Selling out of sequence kills the sale. Even if you do the right things, if you do them in the wrong sequence or order, you will kill the sale. New salespeople with little experience often violate this principle. When they meet with a customer for the first time, they introduce themselves and immediately begin talking about their product or service. Instead of asking a series of well-organized questions to understand the customer's needs, they start making product or service recommendations. As a result, their customers quickly become guarded or back off completely. No trust or rapport has been built. It is clear that the salesperson has no other thought or concern except talking about and selling his product or service. He does not care at all about the customer.

The third part of the new model of selling is *presenting your product or service*. In the new model, you carefully match what your customers have said with what your product or service will do. You only talk about things that your customers have said are of concern to them. Like a hand into a glove, your solution should fit their expressed needs. You would say to the customer, "You mentioned that you had this need or concern. Well, our product or service satisfies that particular need in this way."

It is said that objections are what you get when you stop talking about things the customer cares about. As long as you are feeding back the customer's words and concerns in your presentation, the customer will listen with total attention.

There is a rule in communications that says, "People do not argue with their own data." If you are talking about your product or service from your own point of view, your prospect can argue and disagree repeatedly. However, if you are feeding back your customer's words in your presentation, the customer cannot and will not argue with you. Customers love to hear their thoughts and concerns reflected back by an intelligent, experienced salesperson like yourself.

The fourth layer of the new model of selling, the triangle at the bottom, is *confirming or closing*. Fortunately, if you have built high levels of trust by focusing on identifying needs and how you can help your customers improve their lives or work, and you have shown how your product or service accomplishes this goal, the close of the sale is usually quite easy. Sometimes it just happens naturally.

At the end of a good presentation, if you have followed all these steps, the customer will very often say, "Well, it sounds good to me. How soon can I get it?"

Perhaps the height of sales excellence is when your customer agrees to buy your product or service without even asking the price. When you have built a high level of trust, the customer knows that whatever price you charge will be fair and honest. The customer trusts you completely to act in his best interest.

The Keys to Relationship Building

The keys to relationship selling are *trust and credibility*. Your level of credibility—how much the customer believes you and trusts you—is the most important determinant of how much you sell, how fast you sell it, how much you earn, and your entire living standard. Trust and credibility are everything.

There are five steps to effective listening. When you learn how to listen effectively, following these steps, you will be astonished at how much faster you build trusted relationships with prospects, and with other people in your life.

STEP 1: ASK WELL-PREPARED QUESTIONS

Like a good lawyer in court, you need to be prepared with questions that are thought through, written down, and even practiced. Your questions should move from the general to the particular. Your questions should be organized, intelligent, and designed to elicit good information from the customer.

STEP 2: LISTEN ATTENTIVELY TO THE ANSWERS

Lean forward. Be an active listener and encourage the other person to continue to speak. Focus your eyes intensely on the speaker's lips, occasionally moving your eyes up to the speaker's eyes and then back to the lips. And don't interrupt, no matter what thoughts spring to your mind. Initially, this takes tremendous self-discipline. People interrupt because they are nervous, or because they think they have something really important to add. Don't interrupt, for any reason.

Rapt attention is the highest form of flattery. When you hang on every word that the other person is saying, lean forward and watch the other person's face intently, nod and smile, you actually have an emotional impact on the other person. Les Giblin, a communications expert, says that this form of listening is like "white magic." It has an almost miraculous effect on the thoughts and feelings of other people, especially their thoughts and feelings toward you.

It is said that many people have talked themselves out of a sale, but very few people have *listened* themselves out of a sale. Listening is very powerful. When you listen intently to another person, you pay value to that person. You make the other person feel more valuable and important. The person's self-esteem goes up. Even the person's heart rate, blood pressure, and galvanic skin response increase. The more you listen to other people, the more they like themselves and respect themselves, and by extension, the more they like and respect you, and by extension, the more they appreciate and value your product or service.

STEP 3: PAUSE BEFORE REPLYING

Instead of jumping in with your own comments when the person you are speaking with pauses, stop for a few seconds and wait. Pausing is classy. It is an elegant form of listening. It is practiced by polished and sophisticated people. It is very powerful.

When you pause, you gain three advantages in the conversation:

1. You avoid the risk of interrupting people if they are just organizing their thoughts before they continue speaking.

2. You tell people with your silence that you are carefully considering what they have said, which means that what they have said is valuable and important, and, by extension, they are valuable and important as well.

3. You allow the other person's words to soak into you at a deeper level of mind. You actually hear and understand with greater clarity. You hear not only what is said, but also what is not said, which often contains the real message.

On the other hand, if you immediately start speaking after the other person has paused, you are sending the message that you do not really care about what the other person has just said. It's been said that most conversation is not listening; it is merely waiting.

STEP 4: QUESTION FOR CLARIFICATION

Herein lies the real art of the conversation, and the key to successful persuasion and selling. Once it is clear that the other person has finished her thought and there's a pause in the conversation, you should assume that you do not fully understand what the prospect really means by what she just said. So you follow up by asking, "How do you mean?"

This follow-on question is one of the most powerful questions that you will ever learn in selling, in any language. Whenever you ask this question of your prospects, you are giving them the opportunity to expand on their previous comment or answer. They will give you more information that can help you to understand their situations better, and to make a better product or service recommendation.

Even if they say something negative, such as, "I really don't feel confident with your product or your company," you can follow up by saying, "How do you mean, exactly?" Then, just wait and listen attentively to their answer.

Here's the key: The person who asks questions has control. The person who is answering the questions is controlled by the person who is asking the questions.

In my book with Ron Arden, *The Power of Charm*, we explained thirty-five different things that a person can do to be perceived as charming in any conversation. Perhaps the most important recommendation is to forget about yourself completely in a conversation and, instead, ask questions and follow-up questions of other people, keeping them talking about themselves for most of the time.

The more you ask questions and listen intently to the answers, the more the other person will trust you. Socially, the more you ask questions and listen to the other person, the more the other person will both trust you and find you to be "charming."

STEP 5: FEED IT BACK

Paraphrase what the customer has said in your own words. Your ability to accurately feed back to your customers what they have told you, in your own words, is the "acid test" of listening. It demonstrates that you were genuinely listening and paying close attention to what the customer was sharing with you. It is only after you have accurately reiterated the customer's problems, concerns, and goals, and the customer has confirmed and agreed that you have an accurate understanding of the situation, that you can begin presenting your product or service as the solution.

In my own business, I will often spend time with my prospective client on the phone or in person asking questions to gain a complete understanding of his problems and needs. I will then write and send a proposal to my client that consists of basically three paragraphs. You can use this same method yourself if you do written proposals to sell your products or services.

In the first paragraph, I thank the prospective client for taking the time to speak with me and share his thoughts and concerns about the situation. I start off the second paragraph by saying, "Based on our conversation, it is my understanding that . . ." Then I go on to explain clearly and in detail what I perceive to be the customer's situation, problems, goals, needs, and concerns. This extended paragraph often takes up 50 percent of the letter or proposal.

Third, in my concluding paragraph, I say, "I believe that I can do a wonderful job in helping you solve these problems and achieve these goals in our two-day strategic planning program that I would organize and conduct for you. I am very much looking forward to working with you in the weeks ahead."

I may add a little more detail about my service offering, but it is usually short and sweet.

Each time I have used this three-part written proposal process, I have immediately received confirmation from the client and a go-ahead with the assignment. As soon as I have made it clear that I "understand the customer's situation," the sale comes together quickly and easily.

In sum, to build high-quality relationships, you should follow a simple process, over and over again:

1. Ask interested and interesting questions. Intelligent questions must be thought through and planned in advance.

2. Listen attentively when the other person speaks; discipline yourself not to interrupt for any reason.

3. Pause before replying. Become comfortable with silence in a conversation.

4. Question for clarification. Never assume that you fully understand what customers mean by what they have said. Ask follow-up questions.

5. Feed it back. Paraphrase what the customer has said, in your own words, to demonstrate to the customer that you were listening carefully.

Keeping the Relationship After the Sale

Customer psychology has some interesting twists and turns. The sale actually begins when the customer says "yes." This is why professionals do not think in terms of "closing the sale" but rather of "beginning the relationship."

As far as the customer is concerned, the decision to buy is actually the *beginning* of the sales process, not the end. And very often, immediately after making a buying decision (especially for a large-dollar item), customers go into a "motivational dip," or what is often referred to as buyer's remorse.

Right after buying, as soon as they get the signed contract and hand over the check to you, customers start to wonder if they have made the right decision. They begin thinking about the amount of money they have paid, the difficulties of implementing your solution or learning how to use your new product or service, and all the things that could possibly go wrong. At the bottom of this emotional dip, customers can lose their confidence and think about canceling the sale. This is why there is a seventy-two-hour waiting period after people buy something where they are legally capable of changing their mind.

When your customers make the sales purchase, they will often start to worry and "catastrophize" about having made a mistake. At this point, they will reach out to the salesperson, like a drowning man grabbing for a life preserver in the ocean. Your customer will phone you, sometimes on the weekend, and say, "I really have to talk to you about something."

This is natural and normal. What the customer needs at this time is positive reinforcement. The faster you respond to the customer's feeling that he has made a mistake, the greater confidence the customer will have in you, and the greater the likelihood that the sale will stay together indefinitely.

Another aspect of buyer's psychology is that when customers make the decision to buy from you and have given you a signature or a check, they may feel that they have done you a favor. Your emotional bank account with the customer is now in a deficit position because the customer thinks you owe him one. This sentiment may be unspoken, but if you do not immediately do something to reciprocate for the customer's decision to buy from you, the customer may feel a bit unhappy, even irritated. In this case, immediately do something to reassure the customer that he has made a good decision. At the very least, send an e-mail the same day. Send a thank-you letter. Send a handwritten card, expressing your appreciation to the customer for doing business with you.

Even better, send the customer a gift of some kind. In our company, we send out gift baskets with delicious gourmet foods to our clients immediately after we have done business with them. Whatever you send, take a little time to make sure that all the ingredients in the gift basket are of truly high quality. It is amazing how many gift baskets, although beautifully packaged, contain foods that normal people would never eat.

Some time ago, a local gift basket manufacturer approached us for our business. We agreed to give them a try. Right after completing an assignment with an important client, we sent the client a big gift basket from this new supplier. To our shock and amazement, the gift basket was sent back to our office with a note saying, "The ingredients in this basket are of such poor quality that we cannot accept them." When we took it apart and looked at the contents, we saw that the customer was completely correct. It was full of old salami, old cheese, old crackers, and cheap candies, but it was beautifully packaged and quite expensive. We never used that gift basket supplier again.

Finally, once you have made an important sale, set up a regular schedule of communication and callbacks. If it is a small customer, you can send out an e-mail or a company newsletter once a month. With medium-size customers, you can send a written thank-you notice or information newsletter every month and call on them personally every six months. With larger customers, you might want to call back on them once a month or once every two months.

The best solution is to tell customers that you would like to keep in touch with them. You can ask, "How often would you like me to call on you personally? What would you be comfortable with?" Customers will usually tell you how often you need to keep in touch with them to keep the relationship and to keep the plate spinning. You can also alternate with e-mails, telephone calls, and personal visits. This is a matter of your own judgment as to what would be the appropriate type of contact.

Become a Relationship Expert

Everything today in selling is relationships. Top salespeople are relationship experts. They know that the quality of the relationship is determined by the amount of time and energy that they invest in that relationship.

You, too, must become a relationship expert. Always look for ways to reassure your customers that the relationship is important to you. The more emphasis you put on your sales relationships, the more sales you will make and the more successful you will be.

There are entire industries where your ability to create and maintain genuine relationships will determine your income: insurance, wealth management, accounting, and real estate are just a few.

Every sale is actually comprised of three smaller sales. The first sale you make, and the most important, is the one in which you sell yourself. No other ability will be more important in any career. In fact, successful salespeople are there at the top because they have mastered the art of selling themselves.

The second sale you make is for time. Before you ask your prospects to pay in money, you must first ask them to pay attention. The key idea is that, in the first contact, selling for time is much easier than selling for money. In fact, one of the biggest mistakes sales professionals make is to start talking about their product or service before they have successfully closed the prospect on an appointment, which is a commitment of time and attention.

Finally, the third sale is the actual sale of the product.

Tip: You can't fake a genuine relationship, so don't try. Find something you genuinely like about your prospect, even if it's a mutually enjoyable activity like running or golfing. Find an area where you have something in common and focus on what makes you similar to each other. If you can't find something you both agree on and like, it will be difficult to create the level of trust necessary to make the sale. Be prepared to move on and find someone else. There are few things worse than trying to build a sales career selling to people you don't like and who don't feel anything in common with you.

—MT

ACTION EXERCISES

Now, here are some exercises, including questions you can ask and answer, to apply these ideas to your sales activities:

1. List three ways to increase the "friendship factor" in each sales relationship.

2. What are the three most important parts of your company's reputation in your marketplace?

3. List three reasons customers are reluctant to enter into sales relationships with new salespeople.

4. Why is the relationship more important to the customer than the product or service in a competitive market?

5. What are the three most common reasons for lost sales?

6. What are the three most common words or expressions customers use to describe top salespeople?

7. What are the three most important benefits that a customer enjoys in a high-quality relationship with the salesperson?

Finally, what one action are you going to take immediately as a result of what you have learned in this chapter?

CHAPTER FIVE

SELLING CONSULTATIVELY

What you get by achieving your goals is not as important as what you become by achieving your goals.
—Wolfgang von Goethe

THE HIGHEST-PAID and most successful sales professionals are positioned in their customers' accounts as friends, advisers, and consultants. Consultative selling is more than developing good relationships with customers. It requires positioning yourself as someone who has the experience and insight to help customers meet their needs.

The practice of the consultative selling approach will help you to move to the very top of your field. It is a valuable tool that is indispensable in dealing with complex sales and accounts where many factors are involved and competition is a key factor.

Although experience and knowledge are keys to consultative selling, the process begins with your personal appearance. If you don't look professional, you will never convince customers that you are indeed the best person to help them resolve their problems.

The Importance of Image

People are extremely visual. Ninety-five percent of the first impression you make on another person is determined by your clothing. This is because your clothing generally covers 95 percent of your body.

My father was a carpenter. The only suit I ever had as a kid was a cheap rental that I got to attend my high school graduation ceremony, even though I did not graduate. I worked at laboring jobs for several years and then got into sales. Because I had no money, I wore the same clothes as a salesman that I had been carrying with me in my backpack.

After I had made a few sales, I was able to buy better clothes, but not much better. I wore a shirt that I washed out in the sink at my boarding house each night. I had a single brown clip-on tie. My shoes were too big for me, so they flopped when I walked, and, besides, they had holes in them.

It did not occur to me until much later that my appearance was sabotaging me every time I approached a prospect.

When I got a job selling mutual funds door-to-door, I bought a cheap suit that looked as if I had bought it from a used clothing store. My shirt was not always ironed, and I didn't know how to tie a tie. Nonetheless, I persevered and began to make more sales and more money, in spite of my appearance.

One day, a friend of mine asked me politely if I would be open to some feedback on my dress and appearance. Fortunately, I was an eager student of self-improvement. When I told him I knew nothing about proper business attire, he sat me down and gave me a complete explanation of the importance of dress in building credibility and conviction in your customers, the various kinds of dress, and the things to look for in a suit, slacks, ties, shirts, and shoes.

That was a turning point for me. He took me to a tailor and arranged to have the tailor make me a bespoke suit, one custom-designed for me, from the initial measurements and the selection of fabric to the completed and fitted suit. When I finally tried it on, I was shocked at the way I looked in comparison to how I had looked before.

My sales took off. I sold more and more, and at higher and higher levels. Soon, I was selling to the senior executives and even the presidents of larger and larger companies. I received recommendations and referrals and was passed from customer to customer. Soon after, I became a sales manager, recruiting and training financial consultants in six countries.

Today, it is very much as if we have reverted to the dressing habits and customs of poor people in third-world countries. People wear jeans and even undershirts to work. They wear shorts and flip-flops. They are not particularly well groomed or properly shaven. They wear open-necked shirts that often are not tucked in at the waist or buttoned at the wrists. And since people who dress like this associate with other people who dress like this, their general impression is that "everyone dresses like us."

But this is not true. The most important factor in sales is *credibility*. Credibility means that people believe you and trust you and are confident that your product or service is good for them and that you will fulfill your promises and deliver what you said you would. Credibility is everything.

The fact is that people *select* the clothes that they wear each day. The clothes you select to wear are a definite and deliberate expression or statement of the person you think you are, your self-image. You dress to tell the world: "This is me! This is the person I am, like it or lump it!"

The key to correct dressing is simple. It goes back to the law of cause and effect. Look at the most successful and highest-paid people in your field, and pattern yourself after them. In neurolinguistic programming, it's called "modeling." When you pattern yourself, in appearance and behavior, after the most successful people in your field, you soon begin to walk, talk, think, and act the way they do. In no time, you will be getting the same results that they do as well.

The second part of image has to do with your grooming and personal accessories. The rule is simple. Dress like a winner. Dress like a professional. Dress like someone that a customer can confidently take advice from because you look excellent in every way.

Qualities of Consultative Salespeople

In the last chapter, we talked about the perception that customers have of the top salespeople in every industry. They describe the salesperson in terms such as, "He works for me," and "I view her as a consultant or adviser," and "He really understands my situation."

Next to your total appearance, especially in the first meeting (which largely determines if there is going to be a *second* meeting), your behavior or demeanor creates the perception of you as a trusted adviser or consultant. Zig Ziglar once said, "If you want people to accept your advice, dress like the people from whom they already take advice."

To be perceived as a consultant, to be trusted, you must act like a consultant in everything you do. Tell the prospect that you are a consultant rather than a salesperson. Come to the meeting fully prepared. Ask good questions, listen attentively, and take careful notes.

Here's a rule: You can be happy, cheerful, and easygoing when you talk about general subjects of interest to the prospect. But as soon as you switch to talking about the customer's problems, needs, or goals, you must immediately become serious, thoughtful, and attentive. You must behave as if you were a "doctor of selling" and the prospect (patient) has now begun to tell you about his pains and why he is there in your office.

Three Types of Customers

Consultative selling requires that you think of yourself differently, and that you position yourself differently in the account. Especially in B2B selling, you must focus on the *financial* results of your product or service, rather than the performance or price relationship. The focus on financial results is the difference between consulting and vending. It is the difference between the perception of you as a business adviser as compared to a salesperson who is just trying to sell a product or service.

Customers are concerned about one of three factors:

1. At the lowest level, the customer is concerned with the performance of your product or service. Will it work? Will it do the job? Will it help me to do my job better?

2. At the second level, the customer is concerned with the price and getting the best deal for the company. That's no different from how a sales manager is concerned about getting the very best sales training for his team at the lowest possible price, or how you as a salesperson are concerned about whether sales training will help you increase your sales effectiveness and income.

3. At the highest levels of business, the decision maker is concerned only about the financial impact of the purchase on the business overall. My friend Tony Parenello calls this person "VITO" (very important top officer). When you talk to this type of person, you describe everything

about your product in financial terms and how your product or service will impact and affect the bottom-line profitability of the organization.

It is almost as if each of these three different decision makers speaks a different language in evaluating a product or service. Whichever of them you are speaking to, you must speak in the same language that he does.

Do Your Homework

The key variable in consultative selling is your knowledge of the customer's business processes. A doctor cannot give advice or recommendations for prescriptions or treatment without first doing a thorough examination, complete with tests, to determine exactly the malady that the patient is dealing with. It is the same in business. You must do your homework. You must learn everything you can about the customer's business before you even dare to suggest a solution or course of action. Remember the saying, "Prescription without accurate diagnosis is malpractice."

In selling to businesses, you must learn how sales are generated. What are the primary products or services sold by the customer's company? How much are they sold for? What is the total sales volume? What kind of sales results are they enjoying?

You should then understand the costs of operating the business. For every organization, the relative distribution costs will be different. In some service businesses, the primary costs of operation are salaries, wages, benefits, and bonuses. In other businesses, it could be the costs of raw materials to produce the product itself.

Especially, you have to know how *profits* are generated. What has to happen for the business to earn a profit, and how can you provide your own product or service in a way that increases profits for the customer?

Define the customer's problem or opportunity in dollar terms. Once you understand the sources of sales, costs, and profits, you offer specific help and advice to improve in one or more of those areas. How much can be gained or lost by using or not using your solution? Never forget that the greatest motivation for buying your product or service will always be improvement, especially financial improvement.

Be a Financial Improvement Specialist

People in business want to achieve one of two things. They want to save or gain time or money. And they want to achieve this goal in a cost-effective way, which means that the solution costs substantially less than the immediate, measurable, and desired benefits that the customer seeks.

The essence of B2B selling is a focus on cost-benefit decision making. Your initial goal is to discover a definite problem that the customer has that your product or solution can solve. The starting point of this process of discovery can be as simple as asking the customer, "What are your main business goals today, and what is holding you back from achieving them?"

Or you can ask, "What is or are the biggest problems that you are dealing with in today's market?"

Go slowly. Never assume that the first problem or difficulty that the customer describes is the real problem or the most important one. Keep asking additional questions. Keep probing. Keep seeking to understand the customer at a deeper level.

Once you are clear about a problem your prospect is dealing with that your product or service can solve, your next goal is to discover the cost of that problem. You ask:

What is that situation costing you?

How much does it cost your business when that problem occurs?

What are the additional costs to yourself and your business if and when that problem persists?

At this stage, you are both a consultant and a "problem detective." You are looking for a customer problem that costs so much that the cost of your solution is only a fraction of the potential financial benefit that the customer will receive by purchasing your services. Your job is to show the customer that, for *this* amount of money (the price of your product or service), the customer stands to gain or save *this* amount of money—in other words, you show the financial benefit of what you offer.

In simplest terms, as a consultative salesperson, you are a "financial improvement specialist." You are seeking opportunities where your solution can bring about definite and measurable financial improvements that are greatly in excess of the amount you charge to provide your solution. Your product or service is only the means to the end—the goal of financial improvement. Most customers have little interest in the details of your solution. What they want to hear about are the results, benefits, and outcomes they will enjoy if they implement your solution.

Practice the 90/10 rule as a financial consultant and adviser. Spend 90 percent of the time talking about the benefits and results of what you sell, and only 10 percent of the time talking about your systems and processes. This is the correct weight of concern or interest in the mind of your customer in almost every case.

Show the Expected Rate of Return

In the early days of computing, when mainframes were a huge, expensive mystery to most businesses and organizations, IBM came up with a simple sales model for selling many billions of dollars' worth of computers worldwide. It was called the internal rate of return (IRR) method.

The IBM rep/consultant would develop a high-quality relationship with the client, based on developing a thorough understanding of the business's processes, and then ask, "How much of a return do you need to achieve to justify borrowing money to make a purchase?"

This was a great question! If the company could borrow money at 5 percent a year on its lines of credit, or by issuing bonds, it would have to be convinced that it could deploy that money in the business and earn a much higher return, for example, 15 percent.

So, the IBM rep would say, "If you could achieve a 15 percent return on investment to your bottom line from one of our computers, you could justify borrowing the money to purchase it, right? Based on our analysis of your business, and the increases and improvements in efficiency and output, we can project that this computer will generate a 25 percent internal rate of return. This means that it will pay for itself 100 percent in four years. With an expected operational life of ten years, after four years, you would be earning a 25 percent net profit, after all costs, on this computer. How does that sound?"

When you can demonstrate to a customer that your product will pay for itself quickly and dependably, and then generate a net profit for a considerable time after it has paid for itself, and that the cost of borrowing the money to buy your product is substantially less than the expected annual return, the sale almost takes care of itself.

Each customer has four questions, usually unspoken, that you must answer in the course of your sales discussion. The four questions are:

1. *How much in?* How much, exactly, will I be required to pay to acquire your product or service?

2. *How much out?* Exactly what return will I enjoy from installing your product or service?

3. *How fast?* How quickly will I enjoy the financial results you promise?

4. *How sure?* How can I be sure that I am going to get the financial results that you promise?

Those are the questions every customer asks: How much in? How much out? How fast? How sure? Be prepared to answer each of these questions in a persuasive way to get the sale.

Accept Responsibility for Results

One of the keys to making business-to-business sales is to accept full responsibility for implementing the solution and getting the results that you are promising the customer. This approach has rapidly replaced the older model, where the consultants came in, did their analysis, put together a report with recommendations, dropped off the report, picked up their check, and left, often never to be seen again.

Today, the best management consulting companies in the world, companies like Bain and McKinsey, not only conduct a thorough analysis and make recommendations, but they accept the responsibility for working with the company to implement their solutions to get the results that they had promised. They are very clear about demonstrating that what they provide is "free, plus a profit."

In consultative selling, you position yourself as a partner with the customer. Show that you have mutual rather than opposing interests. Focus on cooperation rather than competition. Focus on collaboration rather than confrontation. Continually use the words *we, us, our* in your discussions. For instance, you would say, "Based on our discussion, I think that what *we* are dealing with today is this. What *we* need to do is that. *Our* biggest concern is this."

Create Your Positioning

There are certain keywords that your prospects and your clients use to describe you when they view you as a consultant rather than as a salesperson. In every interaction with your client, you should look for ways to demonstrate and reinforce these particular perceptions:

1. *Expert.* Clients prefer to deal with people who are experts in their particular problems, needs, or circumstances. The more time you invest in studying and understanding their industries and giving them valuable ideas, the more they see you as an expert.

2. *Knowledgeable.* By reading trade magazines, using Google to research keywords, and keeping current with the industry in which you are selling products or services, you can engage in intelligent conversations about the industry with your clients.

3. *Adviser.* Instead of trying to sell or persuade your client to buy a product or service, you give advice in the form of suggestions and recommendations ("What I recommend that we do now would be this . . .").

4. *Friend.* The key to positioning yourself as a friend is to genuinely like and care about your customer. You must be friendly and cheerful, and you must ask good questions and listen to the answers.

5. *Helper.* As a helper, you are constantly looking for ways to help your clients to improve their situation, usually to

reduce costs, increase profits, and/or generate greater efficiencies.

6. *Problem Solver.* In the final analysis, this is a complete description of your role in the customer account. Just as a medical doctor seeks symptoms and maladies, as a doctor of selling, you look for problems for which your products or services are the ideal solutions.

7. *Questioner.* The best consultants ask at least twice as many questions as they make comments. Sometimes, all they do is ask questions. Peter Drucker once said, "I am not a consultant; I am an insultant. I do not give advice; I merely ask hard questions that force my clients to think with greater clarity."

8. *Listener.* This is one of the best perceptions that you can create in the mind of your client or prospective client. In study after study, the most successful salespeople were rated as being "excellent listeners." No top salesperson was ever described as being a "great talker."

Earn the Right

Positioning yourself as a consultant in the sale is essential to your success. You must earn the right in advance by doing thorough preparation. Study your prospect's company in advance of your first meeting. This first meeting is your very best opportunity to demonstrate that you are the kind of person that customers can confidently proceed with.

Have information and ideas to trade with the customer for more information. For instance, you might share an observation that "according to the research that I have done, your industry is going through three major transitions: They are this, that, and the other. How is your particular company positioned with regard to each of these three transitions?"

Seek a win-win relationship with the customer. Show customers that you are genuinely concerned about helping them to improve in the key result areas that are most important to them and their particular positions. Always look for ways to help customers to achieve their goals with your product or service. And the way you do this, always, is to ask well-prepared questions and then listen intently to the answers.

Consultative selling moves you into an entirely new category of sales professionals. It takes you away from the continual contest and argument over costs, price, and performance. When you focus your attention on showing customers how they can financially profit from the use of your product or service, you'll achieve sales results above anything you have yet imagined.

Position yourself as an authority by educating your prospect or client. There may be a better way to build trust, credibility, and deliver value all at the same time, but it hasn't been discovered yet.

Find an opportunity to educate your clients on their business, industry, or a new and relevant technology. Your superior knowledge, and your ability to share it, will immediately make you valuable to the customer. Also, a well-delivered lesson can make your product or service seem indispensable.

I have sold technology products in a competitive environment where the only differentiator was the time I spent educating the customer on best practices, industry status, and strategy. When you teach your customers how beneficial your product or service can be, they will buy your total solution: your product, your company, and you.

Here is a simple format that will change your sales conversations:

1. **Tell them the story of your company.** *The operative word here is "story." Keep it simple; start at the beginning. Describe the key players and their backgrounds and personality traits. Use the first names of your colleagues. Answer the "why?" question: Why was the business started? What problem are you trying to solve? How did your company develop? What were your main milestones in developing your solution? Describe one or more of your existing customers and the value you are delivering to them. Refer to the future and how your product can help your prospects to achieve more of their goals cost-effectively. Describe your most exciting project and the benefit your customer is getting from using what you are selling.*

2. **Tell them about the people who created your product or service.** *If you don't know who the original inventors are, find out. Stories are a time-tested format for delivering information, lessons, and entertainment. Humans are hardwired to listen to stories, not sales presentations.*

3. **Describe why your company, your people, and your product or service will fit well with your prospect.** *Once your prospect understands the context of your company and its people, it will be hard for a competitor to seem more attractive, even if the competitor is offering something that you don't have. Be sure to tell customers that you really want to do business with them. Your obvious desire to have them use and benefit from what you are selling can be very persuasive when they make the final decision.*

—MT

ACTION EXERCISES

Now, here are some questions you can ask and answer to apply these ideas to your sales activities:

1. What three things can you do to position yourself as a consultant in the mind of your prospect or customer?

2. How are the top 10 percent of sales professionals described by their customers?

3. What must you focus on and talk about to be perceived as a consultant by your prospects and customers?

4. In what three ways does your product or service improve the financial situation of your customer?

5. What three things can you do to become more knowledgeable about your customer's business processes?

6. How can you quantify the bottom-line results of using your product or service?

7. What steps can you take to position yourself as a partner with your customer?

Finally, what one thing are you going to do differently in your sales activities as a result of what you have learned in this chapter?

IDENTIFYING NEEDS ACCURATELY

Nothing splendid has ever been achieved except by those who dared believe that something inside them was superior to the circumstance.
—Bruce Barton

CUSTOMERS BUY for their reasons, not yours. The most important thing you do in the questioning phase of a sales presentation is to uncover the true needs or problems of the prospect that your product or service can fulfill or solve.

Selling is both a science and an art. Top salespeople have a set of skills they can use to establish higher levels of rapport and to separate prospects from suspects. By learning and practicing a series of powerful, proven skills used by high-performing salespeople everywhere, you can dramatically increase your effectiveness and your results. In this chapter, you will learn some of the best ideas used by some of the most successful salespeople to identify needs accurately.

Ask Questions Focused on Problems and Needs

The key to sales success, in every situation, with every customer, is to ask intelligent questions and listen closely to the answers.

Be a student; let the customer be a *teacher*. Imagine that you had an opportunity to study your favorite subject under the world's greatest expert or authority on that subject. You would be in a small class with the guru, who would be sharing with you precious insights and ideas that were not available to anyone else. How would you behave? My guess is that you would be on time and thoroughly prepared, and that you would listen intently and take careful notes from everything that the master teacher said.

You should view your prospects the same way. They are the experts on their unique situation. They are the gurus about their companies, problems, or needs. They are the recognized authority on the use or nonuse of your product or service. Your job is to treat the customer as a person having the specialized knowledge that you are interested in acquiring.

Problem- and need-focused questions uncover selling opportunities. The more questions you ask and the more you listen to the answers intently, the more likely it is that you will uncover opportunities, some of them unexpected, to sell your product or service.

Prepare your questions in advance. Consider the wording carefully. Francis Bacon wrote, "Writing maketh an exact man." In selling, you should write out each question and study the wording of that question to make sure that it is framed in the best possible way. Sometimes, small changes in the wording of a question can elicit much better responses from your customer that can lead to sales that you did not anticipate.

Rehearse your sales questions with your colleagues, friends, and family members. Remember, when you meet with a client, you are "onstage." You could not imagine an actor going onstage without thoroughly memorizing his lines in advance and both practicing and rehearsing them over and over again until they flowed normally and naturally.

Adopt the Agenda Close

Use the "agenda close" with each client. This technique takes a little extra time and trouble to prepare, but the results that you will get from it, from the first time you use it, will be quite amazing. Here is how it works: Prepare a list of questions, from the general to the particular, and then type them up on a sheet of your business letterhead. At the top of the page, write the company name and the date and time of your meeting. Just below that, write the words "Agenda for Meeting with _____" and then write in and correctly spell the customer's name. You then write five to seven questions in large typeface (preferably 16 point) and space the questions out down the page so that there is room for the customer to make notes. You prepare this agenda exactly as if you were having an important business meeting with people seated around the table.

When you arrive at your meeting, you say something like, "Thank you very much for your time. I know how busy you are. I have taken the liberty of preparing an agenda for our meeting. These are some questions that we can go over to determine whether my company can help your company in a cost-effective way. Would that be all right?"

Customers love it when a professional salesperson arrives with a written agenda. You then hand one copy of the agenda to your customer and keep one copy for yourself. As you go through the questions, you stay on track, moving in a logical sequence. I call this the "spine and ribs method" of questioning. The spine or vertebrae are the core questions that you have written down. The ribs are the side questions and comments that will arise as you go down the list. Keep accurate notes on the agenda in front of you and on a notepad as well.

The very fact that you have prepared an agenda, and that you work from the agenda, tells people that you respect their time. It also tells your prospects that you are a busy professional. It raises your credibility and increases your self-confidence. It makes you feel and act like a consultant.

Create a Positive Self-Image

Self-image plays a major role in sales effectiveness. The rule is that the way you see yourself on the inside is the way you will be on the outside.

You can actually transform your personality by visualizing yourself as absolutely excellent in what you do. Visualize yourself as calm, confident, and articulate in every sales situation. Visualize the customer as being positive, interested, and eager to learn what you can offer in terms of products and services.

See yourself as a consultant and a knowledgeable problem solver rather than a salesperson. Some consultants earn hundreds of thousands of dollars a year asking questions and giving valued advice to their senior business clients. I have met many of these people over the years. Without exception, they are all dressed and groomed impeccably. They look like a million dollars. You should act, look, and dress the same.

View yourself as a "problem detective," as a person looking for problems for which your product or service is the solution. The greater clarity you have regarding your answers to questions about specialization, differentiation, segmentation, and concentration (the four key strategic thinking principles discussed in Chapter 3), the more and better prospects you will see all around you. Also, read business sections in the newspaper and business magazines or websites to spot prospective clients for your products or services that you may not have noticed before in the absence of a clear definition of your ideal customer.

Become a Doctor of Selling

Be completely professional in everything you say or do. As a doctor of selling, you have a "code of ethics" that you follow with every patient (customer). You treat each customer with respect and professionalism.

By the way, to become professional you must understand the difference between a "customer" and a "client." A customer is someone to whom you sell something. Your relationship is purely *transactional*. You offer a product or service for a specific amount of money and convince the prospect to buy it from you. You then go on to the next customer.

A client is completely different. A client is someone who is under your protection. When Israel is referred to as a "client state" of the United States, it is clear to the entire world that Israel is under the protection of the United States. By the same token, when you start to treat your customers and contacts as if they were your clients, as if they were under your protection, you will treat them differently, and they will treat you differently in turn. When you treat them as clients, continually looking for ways to help, guide, guard, and protect them in making the right decisions, your attitude toward them will change and their attitude toward you will change as well.

As a doctor of selling, you go through three stages in every client meeting, especially the first one. All doctors of all kinds, worldwide, follow the same three steps with every patient, not only the first time, but each time they see that same patient:

1. *Examination.* The first step in the doctor of selling relationship is for you to do a thorough exam of the customer. Let's call this the problem/need identification phase. A doctor won't discuss treatment or prescription options with a patient without making a thorough examination and a diagnosis first. Similarly, you must make no mention of your product or service before having made a complete examination as well. It is not possible for you to reach a professional conclusion and recommend a prescription or course of treatment for your client before you have completed the examination. To talk about your product or service or to suggest features and benefits before you thoroughly understand the customer's situation is a form of "sales malpractice." When you engage in sales malpractice, you immediately disqualify yourself as a serious sales professional (just as a doctor who wrote a prescription before an examination would be engaging in medical malpractice).

2. *Diagnosis.* Once you have done a thorough examination, including asking sufficient questions, you are in a position to identify the exact problem or ailment that your customer is dealing with.

Highly paid management consultants will often interview the client exhaustively, gather large amounts of information, and conduct extensive research and opinion polls, before returning to the client after several weeks with their recommendations. Likewise, once you have assembled your information and results, you return to the client and explain what you have found. You ask the client if your findings are consistent with his experience. It is only when your client agrees that what you have discovered seems to be the real problem that needs to be solved that you can proceed to stage three.

3. *Prescription/Treatment.* This is the stage in the doctor of selling process where you can finally begin talking about your product or service and how it will solve the problem you have identified or satisfy the need that you have uncovered. It is only at this point that you have earned the right to begin the actual presentation and recommendation phase of your customer interaction.

From now on, think of yourself as a doctor of selling, as a highly paid professional whose primary concern is to take excellent care of his patients (clients). The more you see yourself as a highly paid professional, the more professionally you will behave toward your clients, and the more respect and esteem they will have for you. When you behave like a professional, even without telling anyone else, your confidence increases, on the one hand, and your credibility with your customers increases as well.

Gap Analysis: Before and After Selling

Your success in positioning your product or service hinges on your ability to perform an accurate gap analysis. If you see yourself as a detective who is seeking problems or needs that your product or service can satisfy in a cost-effective way, then like a detective, your key to uncovering needs accurately is your ability to ask carefully planned questions and to listen closely to the answers, for both what is said and also for what is not said.

For a customer to buy from you (or to buy anything from anyone), there must be a gap between where the customer is today and where the customer could be with your product or service. The rule is, "No gap? No sale!"

For example, in selling investments, you analyze your client's portfolio and discover that she is earning an average of about 5 percent per year on her total investment portfolio. You show that by reorganizing and reallocating her investment mix, you can achieve an increase of 10 percent per year. The difference of 5 percent is the gap between where the customer is now and where the customer can be.

One of the standard forms of gap analysis is the "before and after" presentation. Think of those television ads about weight loss or fitness products. The thirty- or sixty-second strategy is simple. First, the advertisement opens with a statement or question that immediately gets your attention if you are overweight: "Would you like to be as thin and fit as you used to be? Are you tired of weight loss programs that don't work? Would you like to lose thirty pounds in thirty days?"

The first question is aimed to attract the attention of a prospect for your weight loss solution. In the next few frames, the advertiser tells you about its remarkable product that brings about rapid weight loss. In the next frames, the ad shows people who were overweight before they used this product. Then it shows those same people with an ideal body or figure, having lost all the extra pounds. The ad then repeats the value offering: "You, too, can lose thirty pounds in thirty days! Call the number below and get started immediately."

With the "before and after" presentation, you define clearly where the prospect is today and show where the prospect can be in the future if he acquires your solution.

What is the gap that your product or service fills? Who are the prospects who have a sizable distance between where they are today and where they could be using your product or service? Remember, the gap must be wide enough, and the benefits substantial enough, to motivate the prospect to undergo the time, trouble, and expense of acquiring and using your solution. This is really the key to selling almost anything to anyone.

Your goal is to help customers identify the gap between where they are and where they could be some time in the future, between the real and the ideal. You then expand the gap by intensifying the need. You continually ask, "How much does that cost you?" and "How much does that cost you as well?" Your job is to expand the gap so that the customer's intensity of desire to solve the problem with your product or service becomes irresistible. When your customers recognize that they have a problem, you suggest a satisfactory cost-effective solution to close the gap with your product or service. This is where the sale is made.

Expect Sales Resistance

In selling, some of the most common words you will hear are, "I'm not interested." These words may be the customer's way of telling you that "I am unaware of the benefits of your product or service, of how much better off I can be with it, rather than without it." If there is a definite cost-benefit advantage to using your product or service to solve the problem, resolve the need, or fill the gap that the customer has, and if the prospect says "I am not interested," it simply means that you have not explained your product or service benefits clearly enough, or the prospect has not fully understood the benefits and advantages of your offer.

Very often, though, the words "I'm not interested" are an unthinking, knee-jerk reaction to any commercial offer. Because people are inherently lazy, the customer is too lazy to give any consideration to what you are saying. In most cases, the customer is so busy and involved with work and other responsibilities that he has no mental energy to pay attention to your offer. Therefore, he simply expresses disinterest as a way of getting out of the discussion altogether.

In this case, when you hear the words "I'm not interested," you can use this reply: "That's all right; most people in your situation weren't interested when we first spoke to them. But now they have become our best customers and they recommend us to their friends." This is a way of grabbing your customer by the mental lapels and getting his attention. Very often, when "uninterested" prospects hear that other people similar to themselves have bought your product and are happy with it, they become curious. And curiosity is one of the most powerful selling tools that you can employ.

Occasionally, a customer will use different words, such as "I can't afford it," without knowing anything about your offering. Again, you simply reply by saying, "That's all right; most people in your situation felt that they couldn't afford our product when we first spoke to them. But now they are among our best customers and they recommend us to their friends." This reply often triggers a different response from the prospect—"Oh really, what is it then?"—which gives you a chance to continue talking with the client and, ideally, set up an appointment of some kind.

Sometimes the customer will say, "We're quite happy with our existing supplier." You then respond by saying, "That's all right, most people in your situation were quite happy with their existing suppliers when we first spoke with them, but now they are among our best customers and they recommend us to their friends."

As you see, this is an all-purpose reply to any initial customer resistance. Whenever you say that "most people in your situation felt the same way . . . ," customers are immediately interested to know what other people like them said and felt, and why they eventually became customers of yours.

Just remember, customer resistance is normal and natural. It has nothing to do with you or your product. It simply means that your customers don't know how helpful your product can be to them. If initial customer resistance were true, nothing would ever be sold to anybody, anywhere.

Ability to Pay and Willingness to Pay

Most people feel that they cannot afford a new product or service when they first hear about it. They have what is commonly called "price neurosis," a negative adverse reaction to learning the price of anything, at any time.

But the *ability* to pay and the *willingness* to pay are not the same thing. Most people are capable of paying, either with their own cash reserves or with lines of credit of some kind. Most customers have the ability to get the money they need to buy your product or service if they really wanted it.

Sometimes we ask, "Mr. Prospect, if you wanted this solution bad enough, you could find the money to buy it somewhere, couldn't you?"

In almost 100 percent of cases, prospects will admit that they could buy the product or service if they wanted it badly. The problem is not lack of money; it is lack of desire. It is your job to increase the buying desire to a high enough intensity that the customer really wants to acquire your product or service.

So, most people are capable of paying, but they don't want to. When people spend a certain amount of money, it reduces their freedom and flexibility. It decreases the amount of money that they have available to buy other things. Because we all love freedom and the opportunity to take independent action, we invariably resist any attempt to take our money away from us, no matter how good the reason. Willingness to pay increases as customer desire increases. The more someone wants to buy your product or service, the more creative that customer will become in finding a variety of ways to come up with the money to make the purchase. We'll talk more about the price objection in Chapter 9.

Qualifying Questions

In selling, the person who asks the questions has control. Anyone can talk. Only the true sales professional can ask leading questions that guide the customer, step-by-step, from lack of interest in the product or service to intense desire to know more about the product, and even to buy it.

Ask probing questions that force the prospect to think. We call these open-ended questions because they cannot be answered with *yes* or *no*. They require a more expanded response. As the customer gives you a more detailed response, it opens your eyes to opportunities to sell your product or service. It uncovers gaps that customers may not have known that they had until you asked the question in the first place.

Here are some questions that you can ask:

1. What are you doing in this area right now?

2. How is that working for you?

3. How do you feel about that?

4. What are your long-term goals in this area?

5. What are you trying to achieve, avoid, or preserve in this area?

6. What sort of problems or frustrations are you experiencing in this area?

7. If I could show you a way to greatly improve your results in this area, would you be interested in looking at it?

The more you ask questions about what the customer is doing now, and what the customer would like to achieve in the future, the more you trigger answers and responses that uncover customer problems and needs. The more you ask questions, the more you uncover gaps that you can fill with your product or service. Professional selling is not manipulation. It is a process of discovering the real needs and problems of your prospect, and then showing the person that those needs can be fulfilled with your product or service.

Your ability to ask skillful questions and to then listen carefully to the answers is the true mark of the top sales professional.

*It is imperative that you approach selling **methodically**. Your ability to use questions to uncover needs is an essential skill, but one that requires patience and practice.*

My favorite way of starting a sales conversation is to say, "Tell me about your business." This simple but powerful open-ended statement will reveal more than any one specific question. Whatever the prospect is currently dealing with will normally surface if you open with this statement at the very beginning of the conversation. You can expand this statement with another, such as, "I have read all about your business on your website and have a basic understanding, but I was hoping you could tell me a little bit more about your business."

Have a pen and paper handy to write down everything the customer says, and use this information to ask laser-targeted questions. Prospects and customers are always impressed when you take the time to write down what they say.

—MT

ACTION EXERCISES

Now, here are some questions you can ask and answer to apply these ideas to your sales activities:

1. What three questions would you use in preparing the "agenda close"?

2. In what three ways can you position yourself as a consultant rather than as a salesperson?

3. What three problems or needs does your ideal prospect have that your product or service could solve or fulfill?

4. When prospects say "I'm not interested," what do they really mean?

5. In what three ways can you increase the customer's desire to buy your product or service?

6. What are three benefits or advantages that you gain by asking questions rather than talking?

7. What is the gap that your product or service fills? List three gaps between where your prospect might be today and where he could be if he bought and used your product or service.

Finally, what one action are you going to take immediately as a result of what you have learned in this chapter?

CHAPTER SEVEN

INFLUENCING CUSTOMER BEHAVIOR

*The greatest discovery of my generation is that
people can alter their lives by altering their attitudes
of mind.* —William James

WHY IS IT THAT people buy or refuse to buy? Why do some
people buy quickly and other people take forever to buy, or never
buy at all?

Many years of research in motivational psychology have been
devoted to uncovering the reasons people behave the way they do,
especially in sales situations. All successful salespeople and marketing campaigns have found ways to tap into those underlying
motivations that cause people to react and respond quickly to
commercial messages and sales proposals. The more you know
about how and why people do the things they do, the faster and

easier it will be for you to turn prospects into customers, and then to get referrals and resales that will make you a top producer in your field.

Each customer has deep subconscious needs that must be satisfied before a purchase decision can be made. Your goal is to satisfy as many of these needs as possible, and as soon as possible, from the very first time you interact with a customer.

What Pushes Customers to Buy

One of the most important questions in selling is, "Why do some customers buy faster than others?" Specifically, what are the strategies and techniques that you can use to rapidly increase the speed at which a customer buys from you, from the first contact?

The normal buying process consists of several steps. First, the salesperson contacts a prospective customer, not knowing for sure whether this customer is a genuine prospect or merely a suspect. Next, the salesperson develops rapport and trust with the client, asks a series of questions to uncover the true needs and wants of the client, makes a complete presentation showing that the product or service offering will satisfy the most pressing needs of the client, answers objections, and then asks the customer to take action on the offering.

It is not unusual for this selling process to take several weeks or even several months, especially when selling large, complex products. Some companies project anywhere from three to nine months for the complete sales cycle, from first contact to a signed contract.

There are many sales situations, however, where the extended process of purchasing is short-circuited and takes place almost instantly. The prospect moves from mild interest to a buying decision in a matter of minutes rather than weeks or months of carefully evaluating the decision and comparing the offer with competitors offering similar products and services. What takes place is almost an "instant sale." Why?

A series of "triggers" have been identified and tested over the years, ever since Robert Cialdini's breakthrough book *Influence* was first released. When you learn how to build your sales approach around these buying influences, and learn how to pull these triggers as soon as possible and as often as possible in the sales conversation, you will make more sales, faster than ever before.

Including these triggers—these psychological buying influences—in your interaction with the customer short-circuits the decision-making process and speeds it up dramatically.

The Friendship Factor

Developing a friendly relationship with the prospect is the starting point of triggering rapid buying behavior. As we described in Chapter 4 on relationship selling, people are completely emotional in their buying and decision-making behaviors. They decide emotionally and then they justify logically.

People buy from people they like. People will refuse to buy from people they don't like, even if they desire the product or service being offered. Because the major obstacles to buying are fear, skepticism, and the memory of previous unhappy buying experiences, a friendly salesperson "melts the ice" that most customers feel when approached by a salesperson for the first time.

How can you develop this "friendship" trigger? First, take the time to *build a bridge of commonality* with the prospect. Find something in the prospect's work or life that you also share or experience. It may be that you both have children, or that both of you like a particular sports team, or you share a similar business or political philosophy. When I meet a prospect or address an audience, I imagine that there is a gulf between us. My first job is to build a bridge across that gulf based on something that we have in common, and then to cross that bridge so that the customer and I are on the "same side."

You should also *dress the way your customers dress* if you want to influence them. You want people to think "He's like me" or "She's like me." If you dress above them, below them, or very differently from the way they dress, you may make the sale, but you are putting up an unnecessary barrier between the two of you that increases sales resistance, skepticism, and suspicion.

Another way to build faster friendships with prospects is to *match the customer's voice, body language,* and *breathing patterns.* If the prospect speaks slowly and deliberately, you should slow your rate of speech so that it is synchronized with the prospect's way of speaking. If the prospect leans forward and uses her hands in an animated way, you should pause for a few seconds and then lean forward and use your hands in a more animated way as well. If your prospect is relaxed and breathing slowly, you should take deeper breaths, relax, and breathe slowly as well.

The Power of Reciprocity

Developing a sense of friendship and common interests is a first step in influencing your buyers psychologically. There are other underlying buying influences that will impact the decision of the buyer. One of the most powerful of these buying influences is called the Law of Reciprocity. This law states that "if you do something for me or to me, I will want to do something to or for you."

Human beings seem to have a "fairness gene" encoded in their subconscious minds. This gene causes them to want to "get even" with other people, in a positive or negative way. From early childhood, people strive toward fairness, and they are usually offended by what they perceive to be a lack of fairness.

Whenever you do something nice for another person, that person is unconsciously motivated to do something nice for you in return. If you go out for lunch with someone and that person pays the tab, the next time you go out for lunch, you will insist on paying the bill. You will often insist on an early follow-up luncheon so that you can "get even" with the other person as soon as possible.

It is almost as if we have an account with each person we encounter, and we do not want that account to be in a deficit position. Whenever you do something nice for your prospects, such as bringing them a book, a copy of an article, a gift from your company, or even a new piece of information that can help them in some way, your customer is automatically conditioned to reciprocate.

I have observed situations where the president of a large company will go out of his way to prepare a cup of coffee for a visitor who has come to his office to discuss business or engage in a negotiation. He will ask if the visitor is comfortable, would like a glass of water, or would like to use the washroom facilities. He makes the person feel relaxed and comfortable in his office. Then, when the discussions begin, the other person is far more receptive and open to suggestions and recommendations from the senior executive.

Three Forms of Reciprocity

There are three forms of reciprocity—emotional, physical, and mental. You should look for opportunities to trigger one or more of them in every customer interaction.

- *Emotional.* With emotional reciprocity, the rule is that "if you make me feel good, I'll make you feel good." When you ask questions, listen closely, nod and smile, and treat the other person as if he's important and valuable, you make him feel good about himself. At an unconscious level, he wants to make you feel good about yourself in some way in return. Flowers usually have a positive emotional impact on women. For this reason, a man who wants to impress a woman sends her flowers, and the more he wants to impress her, the bigger and more lavish the bouquets he sends her. When women receive flowers from a man, they automatically feel warmer and more positive toward that man.

■ *Physical.* To trigger physical reciprocity, you use material objects. Whenever you give a gift, a discount, or a worldly favor that improves the person's life or work, that person feels obligated to you and has a deep desire to reciprocate in some way.

■ *Mental.* With mental reciprocity, whenever you give other people an idea, an insight, a method, a technique, or a strategy that they can use to get better results and improve their situation in some way, they feel obligated to you and want to respond.

In triggering reciprocity, the response is often out of proportion to the size of the kindness or favor. You bring him a coffee mug with his name on it, and he buys a $5,000 piece of equipment from you, rather than your competitor.

Because the desire to reciprocate is so strong, and is almost automatic with most people, you should continually look for ways to do nice things for your customers at every opportunity. Each time you do something nice for a customer, you add to your account and build up the desire and willingness of the customer to reciprocate by selecting your products or services.

Strike at the Heart of Their Needs

Another way to trigger the psychological buying influences of your customers is to strike at the very heart of their needs and wants. Every prospect has wants, needs, and goals that can be quite emotional. Whenever you touch upon a genuine need, you trigger an emotional response within the customer to reach out and acquire your product or service.

This is why the process of identifying needs accurately is so important. The more time you take to find out what customers really want, need, and hope for in their lives and work, the more open they are to being influenced by you. Find out the customer's true goals and ambitions, both for himself in his work and in his personal life.

A friend of mine is a very successful salesman of financial and estate-planning services. When he meets potential prospects at a networking event or on a social occasion, he immediately asks them all kinds of questions about what they do, how long they've been doing it, and how much they enjoy it. They automatically reciprocate by showing an interest in him and asking about his life and work. The first and most common question is, "What sort of work do you do?" My friend works exclusively for the owners of small and medium-size businesses. When one of these business owners asks him, "What sort of work do you do?" he answers by saying, "I make work optional for business owners."

This answer immediately pulls an emotional trigger and elicits an interested response: "How do you do that?" My friend then says, "Let us get together for a few minutes and I will show you exactly how I can help you to make work optional. You don't necessarily want to stop working, but you do want to be able to choose to take time off without worrying about your business, isn't that true?"

Making work optional in this way happens to be a primary need, want, and concern of almost all business owners. As a result, they immediately pay attention to him and want to learn more about what he does. By pulling this buying trigger at the first meeting, he leapfrogs over the earlier parts of the sales process.

The customer's main question now becomes, "How can he do that for me?"

When you can describe your product or service offering in terms of the outcome, benefit, or transformation that will take place in the customer's life as the result of acquiring your product or service, you can often trigger an immediate desire in that customer to buy from you and begin enjoying the benefits that you have described.

The Desire for Consistency

The desire for consistency is another major psychological factor in making a buying decision. People strive to remain consistent with what they have done in the past, consistent with their ideal self-image, and consistent with a comfort-zone buying strategy.

Ask prospects about purchases they have made in the past and their reasons for making those purchases; you'll gain some valuable insights. When you then make your presentation, demonstrate that what you are suggesting that the customer do is consistent with how she has bought this type of product or service from other companies.

Customers also try to remain consistent with the image that they have of themselves, especially their "ideal images"—the images they have of the person that they would like to be at some time in the future. Using the right phrases will trigger this desire for consistency. Here are some examples:

- "Cutting-edge companies are implementing this solution in their businesses all over the country." This statement triggers within the prospect a desire to be like those "cutting-edge companies."

- "The fastest-growing companies in every industry are applying this strategy to their business activities." When prospects hear this comment, they have an almost automatic desire to purchase your product or service so that their companies can be among the "fastest growing in the country."

▪ "You're obviously one of the most knowledgeable and experienced people in this industry. Here's what other people like you are doing in their companies . . . ." This type of statement triggers the desire to remain consistent with the qualities that you have just ascribed to the individual. Winston Churchill once said, "If you wish to influence a person's behavior, impute to him a quality that he may not have, and he will strive to demonstrate that quality in his behavior."

Another way to use the buying influence of consistency is to discover the prospect's "buying strategy." Every person develops a method or a process of making particular buying decisions. For example, the average new car buyer visits ten different dealerships, narrows his selection down to three dealerships, and then buys the car he wants from one dealership. Therefore, if you are selling cars, you should immediately ask the prospect, "How many dealerships have you visited?" If the customer says, "This is the first one," it is going to be difficult for you to get him to move out of his comfort zone and make a buying decision before he has shopped around a little bit more. People become comfortable with a particular buying strategy and are reluctant to deviate from it.

Ask your prospects how they have gone about buying products or services like yours in the past. What steps did they take? What factors did they take into consideration? What did they look for? What were the most important elements that convinced them to purchase one product or service rather than another? Whatever the customer tells you, take careful note. Then, structure your offering so that it is in harmony with the way the customer is accustomed to buying.

Whenever you can, point out to your prospects that what you are asking them to do is consistent with what they have done in the past. In this way, their buying resistance will decline and their likelihood of making a buying decision will increase substantially.

Who Else Has Done It?

Another very powerful buying influence—perhaps one of the most powerful of all—is social proof. People are inordinately influenced by other people like them who have bought your product or service. One of the first things that the customer wants to know is, "Who else that I know and respect has bought this product?"

There are several factors that trigger the influence of social proof. People in the same occupations who have bought your product or service can exert a considerable influence on the buying decision. People with the same likes and hobbies as you who have bought your product or service will influence the buying decision. People with the same interests, desires, backgrounds, families, and religious or political beliefs will often trigger the decision to buy from you right away.

Customers are lazy, just like everyone else. They are always looking for shortcuts, especially to buy things that they might want and need. But they have huge psychological obstacles concerning whether the product is suitable, properly priced, affordable, effective, and able to deliver on the results or benefits that it promises. Sorting through these issues takes a lot of time, which is why, in the normal selling process, several meetings are necessary to answer all the objections and concerns that the prospect might have. It is only when your prospects have reached a high level of assurance that their needs will be met in a cost-effective way that they can buy at all.

However, when someone else that the prospect knows and respects has already bought the product or service, the other person, in effect, has done the "heavy lifting." The person who has already bought, it is assumed, has already checked out the product or service to make sure that it is a good choice. Therefore, the customer thinks, "I can safely buy this product or service with no further questions because other people like me already have."

Social Proof Tools

Perhaps the most powerful social proof tools you can use to trigger an immediate buying decision are testimonials of all kinds from people who have purchased the product or service and are happy with their purchase decision.

There are four types of testimonials that can get you instant sales: *letters, lists, photos,* and *videos.* Today, it is so easy to take a video of a happy customer talking about his successful experience with your company and your product or service that you should be recording videos of your customers with your iPhone or other smartphone everywhere you go.

Be sure to ask your happy customers for letters where they compliment you, your company, and your product or service in positive terms. One excellent letter from one customer can dissolve all sales resistance in a matter of seconds. Perhaps the best way to get positive testimonial letters is to ask one of your friendly customers to write it for you. Even better, offer to write the letter for your customer, for him to place on his letterhead with his signature.

With my clients, I encourage them to set a goal of having each salesperson bring one positive testimonial letter from a satisfied customer to the next sales meeting. The company then makes copies of all the letters and distributes one copy to every salesperson to put in a binder in plasticized pages. Use yellow highlighter for the very best words and phrases in the letter.

The next time you sit down with a prospect, you can say something such as, "Before we start, I would like to show you something that we are very proud of. These are letters from our satisfied customers." You then take out your binder and place it in the customer's hands and let him read through the letters one by one. You will be amazed at how many customers will look up from the binder and decide to buy, right then and there.

Another powerful tool to build social proof is a list of happy customers. If you have lists of ten, fifty, or a hundred companies or individuals who have bought your product or service, and especially if the names are well known, you literally demolish any sales resistance the customer might have. If all of these people have already purchased your product or service and are apparently using it satisfactorily, no more thinking about the buying decision is required.

Since people are highly visual, photographs showing your happy customers using or enjoying your product or service are a powerful way to build credibility and lower buyer resistance. Whenever someone sees a photograph of a happy person—especially a smiling face—in an attractive setting, there is an unconscious desire to be like that person, and to be happy as well. This is why so many advertisements for luxury goods, vacations, and resorts show the happy, laughing, and loving faces of people using the product or service. Visuals are powerful ways to lower resistance and increase buying desire.

The Influence of Authority

Authority is also a major buying influence. We are strongly influenced by people who are known and respected for their expertise. When you can mention to the prospect your years of knowledge and experience in this field, you increase the value and importance of any recommendations you make.

On television or in print, when a company wants to sell any kind of medicine or food supplement, the best type of person to recommend it would be a doctor or, better, more than one doctor. You have all seen the advertisement that begins, "Doctors say . . ."

It is quite common to bring an expert from your company to a meeting with a customer. When selling high-tech products, the presence of an experienced engineer or program designer in the customer conversation can be very persuasive.

When selling smaller items, the ideal time to bring in the sales manager (the authority figure) is at the end of the sales process, to give that extra impetus that closes the sale. On the other hand, the best time to bring in the sales manager in a *complex* sale is at the beginning of the process. By having the top person present at the first conversation between the salesperson and the prospect, the prospect is almost always impressed with the value and importance that the company places on the potential of this transaction.

In large, expensive sales of products and services, especially in technology and software, the president can have a major influence on the buying decision simply by showing up to meet with the key decision makers early in the process.

When you can refer to highly respected individuals, especially experts or authorities in the area of your product or service, who can explain how much they believe in the value of what you sell, you are often able to dissolve sales resistance and close the sale immediately.

Buying behaviors are also influenced by *symbols* of success or authority, such as cars, clothing, and accessories. When you visit the customer well dressed and turned out, or when you take the customer to lunch in a new, expensive car, these factors often influence the customer to be more open to what you are selling.

The Power of Scarcity

The relative scarcity of a product or service has a powerful psychological influence on the customer's sense of urgency to take action immediately. Scarcity implies value and desirability. Always suggest or imply that the quantity of your product or service is limited because of its incredible popularity. Tell customers that "people are purchasing this product or service faster than we can fill orders."

Scarcity increases the urgency to make a buying decision. Telling a prospect that there is only one of this item left at this price often triggers the decision to buy immediately.

The Contrast Principle

Contrasting and comparing purchase options is another way for customers to overcome any psychological barrier or concern about the purchase. In strictest terms, potential customers always have one of three choices when presented with a new product or service offering: (1) They can buy what you are selling; (2) they can buy something else from someone else; and (3) they can buy nothing at all. To lower the perception of risk and create the self-assurance that this purchase decision is a good one, customers go through a process of contrasting and comparing in different ways.

> ■ *Cost Comparisons.* Compare the cost of your product or service with other products or services. For instance, you can start with the highest-priced competitive product or solution and then show that your product or service, at a lower price, is as good, if not better. Usually, whichever price you present *second* seems vastly higher or lower than the price you present first. When you say that "the competitor's item costs $100, but ours is only $80," your product or service seems vastly cheaper in comparison. But if you say

that "our product is $80 but their product is $100," the other product seems much more expensive. It is a mental optical illusion.

▪ *Time Comparisons.* Explain the longer amount of time required for prospects to do it themselves or to buy from a competitor rather than to buy your product or service right now.

▪ *Energy Comparisons.* Show the amount of personal energy required to use an alternative product or method instead of going ahead with purchasing your offering today.

▪ *Benefit Comparisons.* Explain the various ways that customers can achieve benefits from a product or service, and then show why your product or service is more likely than any other alternative to give them the outcomes and results that they want. Continually emphasize all the benefits that make your company or product the best choice, especially in comparison with other choices available.

Choose Your Words

A powerful word that will have a psychological impact in the buying conversation is "because." Any reason following the word "because" seems more logical and persuasive:

"You will like this solution *because* . . ."

"This is the best choice available to you *because* . . ."

"This is the one you should choose *because* . . ."

Whenever you have the opportunity, always precede a reason or argument to choose your product or service with the word "because," and then give a good reason.

The word "recommend" is also quite persuasive in a sales conversation. Instead of asking people to buy, make recommendations. "What I would recommend for you would be . . ."

Small changes in the way you present ideas and information can have extraordinary effects on the way your customer reacts to your product or service. You must be continually looking for better ways to present product or service benefits using the buying influences and decision triggers that have been discovered over the years. You will soon be able to turn a negative prospect into a customer with a few simple questions, statements, and actions.

At the Supermarket

You see examples of how these psychological buying influences are used on you and others almost everywhere you go. Every successful sales and marketing effort includes one or more of these behavioral triggers designed to short-circuit an extended buying process and get customers to buy immediately.

Here's an example. You are shopping at the grocery store. Someone gives you a sample of a product to taste. You eat the sample and enjoy it, which automatically triggers within you a series of responses:

- When you eat the sample, you experience a desire to *reciprocate* and a feeling of obligation.

- You begin the process of incremental *commitment* toward buying and using the product.

- You see others around you tasting or buying the product, which triggers the influence of *social proof*.

- The person offering the product is pleasant and friendly, triggering the emotion of liking, which is the *friendship factor*.

■ The product is offered in a store that you patronize, which lends the product the *authority* and prestige necessary to get you to buy it.

■ There is a special offer on the product at this price, which triggers the buying influence of *scarcity*.

■ You *contrast and compare* it with other products and conclude it is a good deal.

Look for ways to incorporate these buying influences into all your sales activities. At the same time, be aware that others will be attempting to use these buying influences on you, everywhere you go. Be alert.

One of the mistakes I made repeatedly in the beginning of my sales career was to assume that if I mastered product knowledge and quickly responded to each objection, I would automatically make a sale. There was an important element that completely eluded me until I discovered it by chance at the end of one very long week. It was 7:00 p.m. on a Saturday, and the sun was going down. I had worked all day with a rep that I was training, and I struck out! I failed to get even one sale. In residential door-to-door sales, you should average at least two sales a day, and more if you are training someone. Alas, I had failed in both areas.

We had a few doors left to knock on before the day ended, so all was not lost—yet. Though we were weary and defeated, I resolved to give the next person who opened the door a great presentation.

We walked up to the door, knocked, stepped back a few paces, and waited. A few moments later a frustrated, middle-aged man opened the door, took one look at our company-branded polo shirts, and immediately went on a verbal rampage, denouncing our product quality and service.

Something came over me, and I snapped. Instead of being low-key and patient, I disagreed with him loudly. I told him that he was wrong. The services that we were selling were in fact different from the services he was describing. He argued back, and so did I. A long technical conversation began that went back and forth for an hour. Happily for us, he actually came around, changed his mind, and bought our services. We walked away with a sale that almost offset the bad day we'd had up till then.

Later, I analyzed my behavior and discovered the element that I had injected into the sales conversation that changed his mind. The missing element was **passion**. I was passionate about correcting his faulty assumption. I truly believed that my product would make his life better.

Since then, I have learned to inject passion into each sales presentation. You can do everything right, answer every question and need, but without passion, no sale takes place. Passion closes the gap. It affects the prospect at an **emotional** level, where most sales are made.

Make sure to pick a product or service you believe in and can feel passionate about. You will be an order of magnitude more successful than if you picked a product merely because you have the opportunity to sell it.

—MT

ACTION EXERCISES

Now, here are some exercises and questions to help you apply these ideas to your sales activities:

1. What are the three subconscious needs that must be satisfied before a customer can make a buying decision?

2. What three things can you do to trigger a feeling of reciprocity and obligation in your potential customer?

3. What three things happen when you do something nice for a customer?

4. Name three ways that you can use the power of "social proof" to accelerate a buying decision.

5. What three things can you do in a customer meeting to get the prospect to like and trust you more?

6. What three things can you say to a customer to trigger the buying influence of scarcity?

7. Give three examples of how the buying influences of reciprocity, incremental commitment, or scarcity are used to advertise and sell products in your city.

Finally, what one action are you going to take immediately to improve your selling as a result of what you have learned in this chapter?

MAKING PERSUASIVE PRESENTATIONS

I am not judged by the number of times I fail, but by the number of times I succeed; and the number of times I succeed is proportional to the number of times I fail and keep trying.

—Tom Hopkins

THE PRESENTATION is the "inner game" of selling where the sale is actually made. It is during the presentation that you transform a skeptical or unconvinced prospect into a committed customer. An effective presentation can increase your sales by several times over an unplanned and uncoordinated explanation or demonstration of your product or service.

During the questioning phase of the sales process (see Chapter 6), where you ask excellent questions designed to elicit wants, needs, desires, and buying ability, both you and the prospect must be clear about four factors:

1. The prospect genuinely needs the product to improve life or work in specific ways.

2. The prospect can use the product and get full benefit from what the product can do.

3. The prospect can benefit from the product in specific ways that are also cost-effective.

4. The prospect can afford the product; it is not too expensive for the prospect's current financial situation.

Once you and the prospect are clear about these four conditions, it is time for you to persuade the prospect to take action.

Develop Presentation Skills

Almost all presentations, up to 95 percent of them, can be improved in some way. The good news is that presentation skills, like all sales skills, are learnable. With a little thought and practice, you can become absolutely excellent at giving persuasive presentations of your product or service. Many of my graduates have increased their sales two and three times in as little as thirty to sixty days by improving the quality of their presentations.

Before you move into your sales presentation, you should restate and agree on the problem or need that you and the prospect have discussed and identified in the questioning phase of the sales process. You then explain why your product or service is the ideal solution to the customer's problem. You should explain exactly how the customer will benefit from your product or service. You should carefully match your product or service features and benefits to specific customer needs. You should ask questions throughout to ensure clarity, to get feedback, and to reach agreement. For instance:

■ Does this presentation make sense to you so far?

■ How does this offer look to you?

■ How does it sound?

■ How do you feel about this offer so far?

■ What do you think about it?

■ Do you have any questions or concerns that I haven't covered so far? (This is a wrap-up question at the end of your presentation.)

Remember, the very best salespeople ask questions continually to keep the prospect engaged, to elicit more information and understanding, to get an opportunity to listen and build trust, and to make sure that they are on the right track.

The Encyclopedia Sales Presentation

A good presentation is carefully designed, rehearsed, and practiced in advance. It is a logical, orderly way of moving from the general to the particular. It is not random and made up as you go along.

There is a famous story that sometime around 1952, a major encyclopedia company commissioned a group of behavioral psychologists to create what came to be known as the "encyclopedia sales presentation." It was designed around forty-two questions, each of which had to be answered with a "yes" for the presentation to continue. The last question was to confirm the purchase and write the check.

As I recall, when the salesman knocked on the door, the first question was, "Do you live here?" This was an important issue to settle at the beginning of the presentation. There was no point in beginning a presentation to a visitor or guest.

The second question was, "Do you believe in the importance of higher education?" If the prospect did not believe in the importance of higher education, the sales visit would stop and the salesman would move to the next house.

Each of the questions became more and more specific, and the presentation proceeded as long as the customer answered these "sweetheart questions" with a yes. Once the sales presentation had been perfected, it was rolled out worldwide. People were recruited by the dozens to go door-to-door, giving this presentation word for word. Because the presentation was so effective, the encyclopedia companies sold billions of dollars' worth of book sets all over the world, and sometimes they sold English encyclopedias to people who did not even read the language.

One of my clients, one of the largest appliance sales companies in the world, developed a similar presentation some years ago and went on to sell many billions of dollars' worth of appliances, cold-calling door-to-door, all over the world. A good presentation can be irresistible, if it is thoughtfully designed, refined, practiced, and rehearsed.

Timing Is Important

Before you begin explaining the benefits of your product or service, and why it is a good choice for the prospect, the person must be interested and curious about what you are selling. Your questioning process in the needs identification phase has aroused the person's curiosity to the point where she wants to know more about acquiring your product.

The environment must also be such that the customer can comfortably pay attention to the salesperson without being disturbed or interrupted. It is the job of the salesperson to orchestrate the timing of the presentation so that the customer can give full attention to what the salesperson is saying.

Proper Prior Planning Prevents Poor Performance

The presentation is to the salesperson as surgery is to the surgeon. It must be planned thoroughly in advance, in every detail. Plan your presentation step-by-step. Review it thoroughly before each presentation. Never take it for granted that you know it well enough.

Many years ago, as an aspiring professional speaker, I was giving the same seminar presentation to different groups all over the country. After the first three or four times of giving the presentation to positive audience response and applause, I concluded that I didn't need to prepare anymore.

The next time I gave that presentation, I walked in without preparing and began talking. What a mistake! To this day, I remember how bad I sounded. I remember the disappointed faces of the people in the audience. Because I had not reviewed my notes carefully right before the presentation, it began to fall apart after a few paragraphs. Soon, people were standing up, shaking their heads, and walking out of the room. I learned my lesson. It never happened again.

Review your presentation before every customer meeting. Never assume that you are so smart that you have memorized it in every detail. Today, even if I have given a presentation a hundred times, I still spend one or two hours before the presentation reviewing every word and every detail before I stand up to speak. The difference it has made in my career has been substantial.

Here's the rule: Preparation is the mark of the professional. There is no such thing as being "overprepared"; the word doesn't exist in the vocabulary of the true professional. Professional salespeople prepare and prepare, and then prepare again. They review every detail of their presentation, and then go over it again. They leave nothing to chance.

The great benefit of thorough preparation is that it allows you to focus completely on your customers. Instead of trying to remember what you wanted to say, you are calm, confident, and relaxed. You feel positive and in complete control. You can focus all your time and attention on your customers and in making them feel good about themselves.

Presentation Methods

Just like a stage play where every piece of furniture is carefully positioned and each actor moves in a prescribed way and says specific things at precisely the right time, your presentation must be thought through and made as effective as possible.

Start with positioning, or where you sit in relation to the customer. Avoid sitting across a desk or table. This is an adversarial or confrontational position, even though it is subconscious. Instead, look for an opportunity to sit kitty-corner from the prospect, or in chairs where there is no table between the two of you. If you find yourself sitting opposite a customer when you are preparing to give a presentation, ask politely if the person would like to move to a place where you would both be more comfortable. In all my years of selling, all over the world, I have never had a customer say "no" to this request.

SHOW, TELL, AND ASK QUESTIONS

Think in threes. People are most happy with information that is presented in threes. It is a special technique that is used by professional speakers for maximum audience impact, and you can use it in a sales presentation.

The very best set of three is called "show, tell, and ask questions." For example:

"This is a new feature that we have recently added to this product." (Show.)

"This is what it does, how it works, and what the benefit is to you." (Tell.)

"Is this something that you would find helpful in your business?" (Ask questions.)

When you show, tell, and ask questions, you keep the prospect totally involved in the sales presentation. Continually solicit feedback by asking questions. The person who asks questions has control.

BECAUSE OF THIS . . . YOU CAN . . . WHICH MEANS . . .

Teach prospects how they can most benefit from using the product or service you are describing. The most powerful way to teach is with another three-step method:

"Because of this . . ." (Describe the product feature.)

"You can . . ." (Describe the product benefit.)

"Which means . . ." (Describe the customer benefit.)

Here is an example: You are selling a flat-screen television and you say, "Because of this flat screen (the product feature), you can mount this television on any wall in your house (the product benefit), which means that you can turn your family room into a theater for your family and friends (the customer benefit)."

Of course, the reason customers will buy is because of the benefit that they will receive. But customers also like to know how they are going to get that benefit, and why. When you use this three-step method of selling, you will be astonished at how readily people buy what you are selling.

I taught this method to a national sales organization some years ago and it was immediately taught to every salesperson in the company. The sales managers told me later that their sales jumped from $50 million a year to $75 million the next year, almost entirely because of the selling and closing power of this three-part presentation method.

THE POWER OF VISUALIZATION

Here is an interesting discovery: It is almost impossible for any customers to buy your product or service unless and until they can visualize themselves actually using and enjoying what it is that you are selling. People must be able to create a clear mental picture of how they will use your product or service. Without that mental picture, they will almost invariably respond with the words, "Well, it sounds pretty good, but let me think it over."

Your job is to create exciting visual images of the prospect enjoying, using, and benefiting from your product. This is why photographs of your product in action are so powerful and pictures of your customers using the product or service are so influential in the sales presentation. It's especially why television advertising is so powerful. As soon as people have a visual image of themselves using the product, they are almost ready to buy.

Think of going to purchase a new car. The very first thing that the salesman does is get you into the car and out for a test-drive. You are ten times more likely to buy a car after you have driven it and experienced it, and have the memory and image of yourself sitting in the car, than you ever would be standing next to it in the lot.

To create this essential visual image, it's very simple: Say the words, "Just imagine!"

"Just imagine yourself using this product or service!"

"Just imagine how you will feel when you start to get the benefits and results from this product or service!"

"Just imagine yourself achieving this result!"

Whenever you say "Just imagine," people immediately create a mental picture of themselves actually doing what you have suggested. As a variation on this theme, you can also say, "Think about what a difference this would make!"

"Think about what a difference it would make in your life if you had achieved complete financial freedom and never had to worry about money again."

"Think about what a difference it would make if every report generated was timely and accurate and you didn't have to go over and double-check them."

Whenever you ask people if they can imagine or "see" themselves using your product or service—"Can you see yourself applying this solution in your work? Can you see yourself enjoying this product at home?"—they automatically create a mental picture and put themselves in the center of it.

GET THE PROSPECT ACTIVE AND INVOLVED

In addition to sitting in a comfortable position relative to the prospect during the presentation, you should get the prospect active and involved. Ask the person to do something. When I was selling, I would ask the prospect to calculate numbers, or to read a particular paragraph in my materials, or to take or give me a piece of paper.

The more physically engaged and involved customers become in the sales presentation, the more likely it is that they will "act themselves" into wanting to actually use and enjoy your product or service. The more active customers are, the more they will see themselves benefiting from what you are selling.

THE TRIAL CLOSE

Use the trial close throughout the sales presentation to elicit feedback. The trial close is sometimes called the "check close," where you check to see how you are doing so far. Sometimes it is called the "signpost close," because you are asking for a signal from the prospect to determine which direction you should go at this time in the presentation. Sometimes it is called the "pulse close," since you are actually taking the pulse of the customer as you go along.

The trial close is the mark of the sales professional. Inexperienced salespeople will often go through their entire presentation, from beginning to end, without allowing or enabling the customer to comment at all. By the end of the presentation, the customer's mind is so overwhelmed with facts and details that he is incapable of making a buying decision. As a result, the customer says, "Let me think about it."

The virtue of the trial close is that it can be answered with a "no" without ending the sales presentation. Instead, it merely gives you feedback that tells you which direction to go and which direction to stop moving in.

For example, you could say, "Do you like this color?" The prospect can say, "No, I hate that color." You can then say, "That's all right. We have lots of other colors that you'll like better."

You can ask, "Would this new feature be something you would use in your business?" The prospect may say, "No, we have no use for that at all." This is a good piece of information for you to have. It tells you to immediately stop talking about the new feature and move on to features and benefits that are of greater interest to the customer.

ALWAYS BE POSITIVE

Successful selling is a "transfer of enthusiasm." The sale takes place when your conviction, your enthusiasm about the goodness and value of your product or service, is conveyed like an electrical arc, from your mind into the mind of the prospect. For this reason, you should be positive, confident, and optimistic about how good your product or service really is, and how good it can be for this customer.

Your level of belief or conviction in the goodness of what you sell exerts a powerful influence on your customer. It is one of the most powerful influences of all.

The most successful and highest-paid salespeople seem to love their products or services, genuinely care about their customers, and are convinced that their products or services can help their customers to improve their lives and work in some way.

Emotions are contagious. When your positive emotion is strong enough, it actually transfers to the customer and makes the customer want to buy and use what you are selling.

Anecdotal Selling

This is perhaps the most powerful part of effective sales presentations. In anecdotal selling, you tell success stories about happy customers who bought this product. When you tell a success story, other customers automatically project themselves into the person of the happy customer and picture themselves enjoying your product or service as well.

The Nobel Prize–winning work on "dual hemisphericity" says that everyone has both a right brain and a left brain. Each of these brains performs very different functions. The left brain is described as linear, analytic, mathematical, practical, fact-oriented, and precise. It is the left brain that carefully analyzes, compares, and evaluates information and ideas. The right brain, however, is completely different. It is stimulated by stories, music, emotions, images, colors, ideas, and people. In fact, the left brain is responsible for learning new words and word meanings, while the right brain is responsible for integrating words and phrases into language.

All buying decisions are made in the right brain. The right brain takes in all facts, figures, pictures, and emotions and integrates them into a single conclusion, to buy or not to buy.

When you create visual mind pictures, and tell stories about successful customers, you stimulate the right brain and trigger buying decisions.

When you are talking to a male customer, tell him stories of happy male customers who have bought your product and the benefits and results they enjoyed from it. When you are talking to women, tell stories about happy female customers who bought and enjoyed your product or service. From time immemorial, stories have been the most powerful way to communicate facts, ideas, and emotions.

Every good story has either a hero or a heroine. When you tell a story about a hero or a heroine, the person listening to the story automatically projects himself or herself into the story as the hero or heroine that you are describing. This is why men like action movies with action heroes and women prefer romantic movies with female stars that they identify with and want to be like.

Who is the hero or heroine in your story? It is the happy customer who bought your product and was better off as a result. Whenever you tell stories about successful, happy customers using your product, you create in your prospect's mind a deep subconscious desire to be one of those people.

Every good story or drama has a villain as well as a hero, which is another use of anecdotal selling. Who is the villain in your story? It is someone who failed to buy your product or service and very much regretted it afterward.

Here's a story: "About six months ago, I called on Bill Smith. He turned me down and decided to buy a cheaper version of this product from our competitor. He called me last week and told me it was the biggest mistake he ever made. He saved a little bit of money, but he had so many problems with the product that now he wants to cut his losses and buy from me, even though our product is more expensive."

When you use dual stories in a sales presentation, you get the greatest positive impact of all. You talk about people who bought your product or service and how happy they were as a result. You simultaneously tell a story about someone who failed to buy your product or service, and how unhappy that person was afterward.

Since your customer wants to be the hero and doesn't want to be the "villain," the customer sees himself buying and using your product or service, and the sale is made.

Plan, Prepare, Rehearse, and Improve

Your goal is to plan and perfect your sales presentation to the point that it is so convincing and persuasive that the prospect buys almost every single time. At the end of an excellent presentation, the customer should be eager to enjoy the benefits of what you are selling. Fortunately, this is largely a matter of thorough preparation and continuous improvement. And presentation mastery is a skill that you can learn.

When I was first trained to sell technical software products, I was handed a series of slide decks (PowerPoint presentations) and told to memorize them. During those initial sales presentations, because I was completely reliant on the slide deck for structure and timing, my communication with my prospects was generally awkward and unnatural.

Slide decks were destroying my ability to communicate effectively, and my sales suffered. Slide decks should play a supporting role in the structure of your sales presentation. Use them as a reference, to reinforce points and provide visuals. Do not rely on a slide deck to present for you. Instead, use the headers on each slide as a general guideline and speak enthusiastically about your product or service. Highlight benefits for your customer and mention case studies. DO NOT read the slides. Your prospects can already read. Your job is to add value to the deck, not be the deck.

The best slide presentations are the simplest. Sometimes a single word and an exciting visual are all you need to convey a great point.

When you design your own slide presentation, I advise that you design two versions. The first deck is the one you present. It should provide a series of great points and impactful visuals that you can explain with passion and enthusiasm. The second deck will be what you send after your presentation. This deck should be designed so that it can stand alone, requiring no further explanation. Imagine it will be sent to ten different people, in different industries or departments. Make it simple and clear enough to be easily understood, especially the benefits the customer will enjoy from using your product or service.

—MT

ACTION EXERCISES

Now, here are seven exercises that you can use to help you to make better presentations in the future.

1. Explain why a planned presentation is more effective than a random presentation that might change with each new prospect.

2. Give three reasons why your positioning in the customer's mind is important in making the sale.

3. What are the three words that customers use to describe top salespeople?

4. What are the three methods of selling used by top performers?

5. List three presentation methods you can use to be more persuasive.

6. What three things can you say to help your prospect to develop a mental picture of using and enjoying your product or service?

7. What are three benefits of using anecdotal selling in your sales presentation?

Finally, what one action are you going to take immediately as a result of what you have learned in this chapter?

OVERCOMING OBJECTIONS

Formal education will make you a living; self-education will make you a fortune.
—Jim Rohn

OBJECTIONS ARE a normal, natural, and unavoidable part of the sales process. Nonetheless, many salespeople become discouraged and disheartened when customers begin to object to their offerings on the basis of high price, better offers from competitors, and other reasons.

The fact is that customers today are bombarded by hundreds and even thousands of commercial messages. As a result, they are skeptical, suspicious, and careful with their time and money.

No matter what you are selling, customers will have questions and concerns that you must resolve before you can proceed to a sale. Your ability to handle these questions and concerns is a key skill that is essential to your sales success.

Back to Basics

The rule is: There are no sales without objections of some kind.

You should always remember three things. First, objections are good; they indicate interest in your product or service. If the customer is sitting there passively, not asking questions or becoming involved in the sales conversation, it is a sign that the person is not really interested in what you are talking about.

Second, objections indicate that you have touched an emotional nerve of the prospect. It is only when the customer has become emotionally involved in your product or service presentation that you have a chance to make any kind of sale at all.

Third, successful sales have twice as many objections as unsuccessful sales. Thousands of sales conversations have been videotaped. What we have observed is that the customer who eventually buys objects far more than those customers who don't buy at all.

When you go fishing and you put out your line, you are hoping that a fish will take the bait and bite on the hook at the end of the line. You are waiting and hoping for a tug that indicates that a fish has taken an interest in your bait. Without that tug, there is no chance you will catch a fish.

In the same way, when a prospect begins to object or ask you questions about your product or service offering, it is the same as tugging at your line. It means that the customer is becoming interested. It means the customer is moving from a position of neutrality and skepticism to a position of interest and curiosity. This is a good sign.

The Law of Six

One of the most powerful principles you can use for identifying and overcoming objections, the Law of Six says that the number of objections to your product or service, whatever it is, is limited to no more than six.

The six objections, or less, that apply to your product or service will be different from that of other products or services. The objections will depend on many factors: your product or service itself, your price and your price relative to your competitors, competitive offerings, the needs of the particular customer you are talking to, the customer's situation politically and financially, and what is going on overall in the marketplace.

When you go out selling and call on customers, you will be amazed at the incredible number of objections that they will give you as reasons not to buy your product. Customers can be incredibly creative. They can think of objections that you cannot even imagine; dozens of them, and even hundreds. But they will always boil down to no more than six major categories of objection.

How do you determine your six major objections? You begin by asking yourself this question: "We could sell to every qualified prospect if they just didn't say . . ."

This is an exercise in sentence completion that you can do alone or with your sales team. It is a powerful technique that is used by companies large and small. Sometimes it is called the "sentence completion exercise." When I do consulting with companies that want to introduce a new product and need a sales presentation, this is one of the first exercises we engage in, every single time.

Make a list of all the objections that you receive in a week or a month, and then divide them into six logical categories. They will usually revolve around your price, the usefulness of your product relative to this customer, your competition, the potential effect or result of your product, the current marketplace, and other factors.

Why or Why Not?

"Why don't our prospects buy our product from us?" This is the key question in determining your most important objections. Sometimes, just by identifying and eliminating one major objection, you can double and triple your sales.

The primary reason that people do not buy is because they do not believe that your product will work to bring them the results and benefits that they desire, in a cost-effective way. To counter this primary objection, you can offer your product or service with a money-back guarantee if it doesn't work. In addition, you can offer a bonus product or service that customers can keep, even if they return your product or service for a full refund.

Many companies use the "risk reversal" approach to selling their products or services. I have personally used this approach throughout my career in selling educational products and services. I say, "Take my product or service. Try it out, use it for thirty, sixty, or ninety days, and if you are not delighted, for any reason, you can return it to me for a full refund."

If your product or service actually delivers on the promises you make to induce the customer to buy it in the first place, you should be able to confidently guarantee customer satisfaction or offer a full refund.

Nordstrom, one of the most successful department store chains in America, offers a lifetime guarantee on any product that you buy from one of its stores. This forces the company to offer only high-quality products and services. People can shop at Nordstrom with complete confidence that they will be able to get their money back if, for any reason, the product or service turns out to be unsatisfactory.

When to Answer Objections

There are four specific times when it is appropriate to deal with objections. The first time is *immediately*. There are some objections you should answer as soon as they come up. This is especially true if your integrity or quality is questioned by the prospect.

If your prospect says something such as, "I hear the products that you sell break down as soon as the warrantee expires," you must address this question immediately. If the customer believes this story about your offering, you cannot proceed. You can say, "Our official warrantee is ninety days, but unofficially, if you ever have a problem with this product or service, we will take care of it or replace it to your complete satisfaction."

When customers have an objection, either spoken or unspoken, it sits in their minds as a block. They think about the objection and fail to focus on your sales presentation. The objection is turning over and over in their minds as they are sitting there looking at you and trying to listen to what you say. If you do not answer the objection clearly and straightforwardly, the lights may be on, but no one is at home.

The second time to answer an objection is *during the presentation*, when the objection comes up naturally or when you bring it up. If you have thought through all the objections you are likely to get and you have developed good answers to them, you will be able to answer smoothly and professionally.

The third time to answer an objection is *later*. Always delay or defer an objection, especially a price objection, until a later time if you possibly can. Price out of place kills the sale. In other words, if the subject of price arises and you begin discussing price before you have created sufficient value in the customer's mind regarding your product or service, the issue of price will become a block in the customer's mind. The person will be thinking about the price so much that he will not actually be listening to you or paying attention to the value that your product or service can provide.

Often the customer will start off by saying, "By the way, how much does your product cost?" Rather than giving the price, you can respond as follows: "That is a good question. I'm going to answer that question completely in a couple of minutes, and I think you will be delighted when you hear the actual price. Can I just finish what I'm saying now and then give you the price in complete detail?" Almost always, customers will say okay and allow you to continue with your presentation.

If you get price questions before you even have a chance to discuss and explain the value and benefits of your product or service, and your price varies depending on what the customer buys, you must make every effort to dodge or sidestep the price question. But if the customer is insistent about knowing the price, you can say something such as, "I have no idea. I don't know whether or not this is even the right product or service for you. But if I could ask you a couple of questions, and show you what we have, I could give you a price that is accurate to within a couple of dollars. Would that be okay?"

The fourth time to deal with an objection is never. Many objections, especially early in the sales conversation, are merely knee-jerk responses and do not need to be answered or replied to.

When the prospect says something like, "I understand these items cost a lot of money, probably more than I can afford," you simply smile, nod, acknowledge the customer's concern, and proceed with your presentation. No reply is necessary. Remember the rule learned in Chapter 8—proper prior planning prevents poor performance. (What I sometimes call the six Ps rule.) The highest-paid salespeople have thought through and identified the objections that they are likely to get and are fully prepared to answer those objections at the right time. You should do the same.

The Preemptive Strike

Use the preemptive strike method to deal with common objections. Anticipate the objection, knowing that the customer is going to bring it up sooner or later. Then bring up the objection before the customer mentions it. Then, answer the objection clearly and straightforwardly so that it is out of the way.

We taught this preemptive strike method to the sales force of a telecommunications company. The company's products were the most expensive in the market. Competitors had taken out ads in the newspaper showing price comparisons so that almost every prospective customer knew going in that this salesperson represented an expensive product.

The sales force was discouraged. They were getting shut down at the first customer contact. When they met with a customer, the customer would almost immediately say, "I know that your products are the most expensive in the market, and I can't afford them. If I'm going to purchase them, I am going to buy them from your competitor, where I know I can get a better price."

We taught the preemptive strike in this way: When the salespeople met with the prospect for the first time, they say, "Thank you very much for your time. I know how busy you are, and before we begin, I want to tell you something. We have the most expensive telecommunications systems in the market today. We are 12 percent more expensive than our second competitor. And yet thousands of companies, like yours, buy our systems every single day, all over the country, even though they know that we are more expensive. Would you like to know why?"

In almost every case, conditioned to respond when asked a question, the customer would say, "Well, yes. Why is it that your products are so much more expensive than your competitors?"

The salesperson would then say, "That is exactly what I am going to explain to you in the next few minutes. I think you will find that it makes better sense for your company to pay more for our products, with all of the associated services that you receive, than to buy something cheaper from someone else."

Armed with this response, the sales force went back out to work. In a down market, their sales jumped 32 percent in the following month. Not only that, one of their saleswomen, who had not made a sale in two months and was thinking of quitting, closed a sale at 10:00 a.m. the Monday after the weekend sales meeting and walked out with a deposit check for $22,000. She was exhilarated.

Remove the Mental Blocks

Each prospect has key objections or concerns that you must get out of the customer's mind and on the table so that you can deal with them. The existence of a single objection in the back of the customer's mind will bring the sales conversation to a halt. You must make it easy for customers to give you any objection at all by complimenting them and making them feel good about objecting from the first moment.

People fear confrontations with other people, for any reason. There may be customers who are more aggressive and assertive, but in general, your customers do not want to fight with you. They want to get along. The easier and more relaxed you can make the sales conversation, the more likely it is that they will share with you the reasons that may be holding them back from buying.

Hear the objection out completely; be patient. Even if you have heard this same objection many times in the past, you should lean forward, nod, smile, practice all your listening skills, and act as if you have never heard this observation about your product or service before.

Remember, if you listen intently without interrupting, pause before replying, question for clarification, and feed the information back to the customer in your own words, you continue to build trust with the customer, even though the customer is object-ing to your offer in some way.

Learn the Right Words

There are several different combinations of words that you can use for answering objections effectively in the sales conversation. The simplest answer of all, when you receive an objection, is to ask your own question: "How do you mean?" Or, "How do you mean exactly?"

This is an all-purpose response to almost anything that the customer says, especially in the case of an objection or concern. This question always causes customers to expand on their previous comments or observations, giving you more information that can help you to make the sale.

You can also say, "Obviously, you have a good reason for raising that objection. Do you mind if I ask what it is?"

Sometimes, the prospect does not have a good reason for the objection. But when you use these words, you are complimenting the prospect and encouraging the prospect to expand on his thought process. This gives you more of the information that you will need to close the sale later.

Answer Objections with Questions

Always answer an objection with a question rather than with an answer. Remember, the person who asks questions has control. If the customer asks you a question, and you begin to answer it, the customer has now taken control of the sales conversation. You are the puppet and the customer is now pulling the strings. You are now verbally dancing for the customer.

How do you handle this situation? Simple. When the customer asks you a question, you say, "That is a good question! Let me ask you something before I respond." You then go on and ask your own question, and then a follow-up question and a further follow-up question. Most customers will immediately forget that they asked a question in the first place, and you will be back in control of the sales conversation.

Discipline yourself to resist the knee-jerk response of answering when you are asked a question. Practice this strategy in your private life as well. Whenever anybody asks you a question, pause, smile, and then turn it around and ask the person a question in return, before you answer.

Remember to use objections as an opportunity to build trust. When you lean forward and listen intently to an objection, and treat customers and their words with great respect, you build trust. You cause the customer to relax and like you more, and thereby become more open to purchasing your product or service.

Dealing with Price Objections

There are several proven ways to deal with price objections, which come up in almost every sale. The first rule to remember is that you never argue about a price objection. You never try to explain or defend. Your prices have been set very carefully by your company, based on a large variety of factors. You can therefore be proud of your prices, stick to your prices, and defend your prices with calmness and confidence.

When the prospect says, "Your price is too high," or "I can get it cheaper somewhere else," you can respond by saying one of three things:

Response 1: Why do you say that? Instead of arguing, your job is to seek the reasons behind the price objection. Where did it come from? Very often, the customer has seen or heard a price on a similar item that is not comparable at all to your offering. Your job is to uncover that information.

Response 2: Why do you feel that way? Whenever you ask people how or why they "feel" about something, they will always respond with an answer of some kind. This is a good question to ask whenever you want to take control of any conversation.

Response 3: Is price your only concern? Especially when customers demand to know the price of your product before you have had a chance to identify their needs accurately and make an intelligent presentation, you must put price in its place. When you ask this question of a customer, the answer you are seeking is "no."

You can say, "Mr. Prospect, I know price is important to you. Could we come back to that in a few moments?"

Sometimes the customer will say, "No, just tell me the price and I will tell you if I am interested or not."

But, as mentioned previously, *price out of place kills the sale.* If the price is variable, depending on what he buys, and you give an estimated price early in the presentation, you will kill the sale. The customer will become completely preoccupied with the price and will have no value to offset it with, or justify it, because you have not yet given your sales presentation.

In a situation where the customer is insistent upon knowing the price, you can ask, "Mr. Prospect, I know the price is important, but let me be clear. Is the price more important than the quality of the product, the installation services we offer, the guarantees and warranties that go with the product, and the follow-up services that we offer you? Is the price more important to you than all of those factors?"

At this point, the customer will often say, "Well, those factors are all important to me, as well as the price." You can then say, "That's great! I'm going to get to the price in a moment, but may I ask you a couple of questions first?" Then, you immediately ask a question, and take control of the conversation.

Here are some other examples of price objections that you may hear from prospects and how to address them with a question of your own.

Prospect: That's more than I was expecting to pay.

You: How far apart are we?

This is an important question for you to ask and answer. If your item costs $1,200 and the customer was only expecting to pay $1,000, you are not far apart. You can find a way to make this work. But if your item costs $1,200 and your customer was only expecting to spend $500, the gap between the customer's expectation and the reality may be too wide for you to bridge.

Prospect 1: It costs too much.

You: How much is too much?

Prospect 2: Can I get this product or service for less?

You: Of course. What part of my offering would you like me to leave off in order to get the price down?

Either of these questions comes as a bit of a shock to the customer. You are forcing the customer to think, in a positive way, which often causes the price concern to diminish and disappear.

The Feel, Felt, Found Method

The "feel, felt, found method" is one of the oldest methods of dealing with price objections, but it is still one of the most effective. When the prospect says something such as, "That sounds quite expensive," you respond by saying these words:

"I understand exactly how you feel."

"Others felt the same way when they first heard our price."

"Here's what others found when they began using our product."

You then give a logical reason why the value and the benefit of your product or service more than justifies the higher price. For instance: "I understand how you feel. Others felt the same way when they first heard the price of this item. But this is what they found when they began using it. They found that it more than paid for itself within the first sixty days and turned out to be a much better deal than a lower-priced product from one of our competitors."

You can even use an anecdote or story about another customer who was concerned about the price but who bought your product anyway, and reported back to you how happy the company was with the purchase decision because of the extra results and benefits that it has been able to enjoy.

Dealing with Price on the Phone

Some years ago, I began selling a new product in the middle of a recession. Business was bad. Cash flow was down. Companies were cutting back. Budgets had been slashed. I heard every reason for not buying that a creative customer could come up with as I phoned prospect after prospect in an attempt to get appointments.

My product was excellent, well priced, and unconditionally guaranteed. It was proven to get results greatly in excess of its cost. I knew that if I could sit down face-to-face with a prospect and show him the benefits, advantages, and guarantees of my product, I could make the sale in almost every case.

But my problem was that I couldn't get past the phone call. When I would get through to a prospect, I would introduce myself and say, "Hello, my name is Brian Tracy, and I'm with the

Institute for Executive Development . . ." Before I could get another word out of my mouth, the prospect would immediately interrupt and say, "How much is it?"

Initially, I would attempt to mollify the prospect by saying, "Well, it's only $295 per person."

At this point, the prospect would say, "I can't afford it!" and hang up.

I knew by now that if I gave the price on the phone, I would be dead in the water. I would never get to see the customer. And getting the initial appointment was the key to my sales success. So I came up with a way of handling the "How much is it?" reaction on the phone.

The next time the prospect asked, "How much is it?" I immediately replied: "That's the best part! If it's not exactly right for you, there is no charge!"

This statement immediately caused the prospect on the phone to do a double take. He would say something to the effect of: "What! What do you mean?"

I would then say, "Mr. Prospect, whatever I'm calling you about, you are not going to buy it unless it is exactly right for you. Isn't that correct?"

The prospect would say, "You're absolutely right!"

To which I would respond, "Well, Mr. Prospect, if you don't buy it, then there is no charge."

The prospect would pause for a few seconds and then say, "All right then, what is it?"

To which I would respond, "That's exactly what I would like to talk to you about, and I only need ten minutes of your time. I have something I have to show you, and you can then judge for yourself." Then I would go on to arrange a face-to-face appointment with the prospect where I could ask questions and make an intelligent presentation.

Eliminate Fuzzy Understanding

In selling, your best friend is clarity. Your biggest enemy is that your customers do not clearly understand why it is in their best interest to buy your product or service at the price you are asking. Most objections arise from fuzzy understanding.

If you have not asked enough questions or made an effective presentation, the problem that your product will solve will not be clear to your prospects. Because they do not understand how your product or service is the ideal solution to their problem, they will have no motivation to buy it. All the customer can see is the price, and not the benefit.

It could be that the *need* that your product will satisfy is not clear to the prospect. Remember, it is perceived needs that stimulate buying behavior. If you have not touched on the nerve of a genuine need the prospect has, the prospect will be neutral toward your product or service and unable to make a buying decision.

The *benefits* of your product or service may not be clear. Customers must feel that the benefits they will enjoy far outweigh the price that you are charging. If this is not clear to them, no purchase decision is possible.

The *unique selling proposition* of your product or service may not be clear to the prospect. Your unique selling proposition is the one benefit or advantage that your product or service offers that sets it apart and makes it superior to any competitive offering. You must first of all be clear about what your USP is, and then you must make sure that your customer is clear about it as well.

It could be that there is *no urgency* for the prospect to take action. The person sees no reason to act now rather than at a later time. Remember: "No urgency, no sale!" Even if people like what you are selling and how you are describing your product or service, if they believe that they can buy it next week, next month, or next year and get pretty much the same thing at the same price, they can punt on the decision. Or, simply to avoid the stress involved in making a buying decision, they tell you that they want to think about it a while longer before deciding.

This is why you must always have a "kicker" in your back pocket; something special that you can offer as a bonus to get your customer to make the buying decision today.

Follow the Formula

The formula for answering objections is simple: *Answer* the objection politely and professionally, provide *proof* in the form of a testimonial letter or something from your sales materials, ask for *confirmation* from the prospect that this answers his question or concern, and then *proceed* with your sales presentation.

Remember, objections are the rungs on the ladder to sales success. The more objections you get, the more interested the prospect is in your product or service. This is a good sign. When you hear an objection, you should be thankful and then begin turning the objection into a reason for buying.

*Practice **objection jujutsu**. Jujutsu directly translated from Japanese means "gentle art" or "flexible technique." It is the martial art developed to fight an armored opponent by using the attacker's energy instead of opposing it.*

To master objection jujutsu, do the following:

- *Do not use any objectionable terms, especially in the beginning of the conversation.*

- *Anticipate and address objections on behalf of your prospects. If they get used to you calling attention to points of contention, they will let their guard down.*

■ *Use the structure of your presentation while interlacing answers to common objections as you go along. The idea here is to skip objections altogether whenever possible and go directly to the close of the sale.*

—MT

ACTION EXERCISES

Now, here are some exercises to help you become more effective at answering objections in the future:

1. What are the three most common objections that you receive when you contact a prospect for the first time?

2. Complete this sentence: "I could sell to everyone I spoke with as long as someone just didn't say . . ."

3. What are the three most common objections that you receive at the end of the sales conversation for not buying what you are selling?

4. What are three ways that you can deal with a price objection, especially when the customer says that your price is too high?

5. What are the three most powerful statements that you use to neutralize objections in the course of your sales conversations?

6. What are three things that you can do to make it easy for customers to object and to express any concerns that they might have about buying your product or service?

7. What are three examples of "fuzzy understanding" that customers might have that would cause them to hold

back from buying your product or service at the end of your presentation?

Finally, what one action are you going to take immediately as a result of what you have learned in this chapter?

CHAPTER TEN

CLOSING THE SALE

Success means having the courage, the determination, and the will to become the person you believe you were meant to be. —George Sheehan

NO MATTER WHAT you're selling or what sales technique you're using, your ability to get your prospect to make a firm buying decision will be central to your success. All top salespeople are excellent at bringing the sales conversation to a successful close. Fortunately, closing the sale is a skill that can be developed, like riding a bicycle. It is simply a matter of learning how to use the right words and ask the right questions, at the right time in the sales presentation.

When you learn how to close easily and well, at the appropriate time, and in the appropriate way, you'll be able to take full control over the future of your sales career.

When I started selling many years ago, going from office to office, I met an endless backflow of sales resistance. I made dozens of calls without making a sale. I sometimes worked from eight in the morning until nine o'clock at night, calling on homes and apartments after the business day, hurrying from door to door, and often made no sales for several days in a row.

My product was inexpensive and paid for itself with one use. My presentation was simple and straightforward. I was positive and enthusiastic. My customers could easily buy my product with no thought, and yet I wasn't making sales.

Of course, like many salespeople, I blamed my lack of sales success on the product, the company, the price, the market, the competition, the economy, and every other factor I could think of.

Not Asking for the Order

When I came to the end of my enthusiastic sales presentation, I would say something like, "Well, that's it. What do you think?"

My prospects almost invariably responded, "Well, let me think about it. Why don't you call me back next week (or next month)?"

I would politely thank the prospect and depart, going on to the next call. Of course, I tried to call them back, but they were always "in a meeting" or "out of town." I never did get a chance to see the prospect for the second time, and none of these presentations ever turned into any sales. It was quite discouraging.

I also learned that the words "Let me think about it" or "I want to think it over" are customer-speak for "goodbye." The customer is really saying, "You failed to ask for the order. I will never think about you or your offering ever again. From the minute you walk out of my office, we will never meet again."

There is a Stevie Wonder song called "Fingertips, Part 2," where accompanied by piano and harmonica, he enthusiastically sings, "Goodbye, goodbye, goodbye, goodbye, goodbye, goodbye,

goodbye!" Whenever a prospect says "Let me think about it," you should hear the refrain from that song rising in the background. You should hear the words *Goodbye! Goodbye! Goodbye! Goodbye! Goodbye! Goodbye! Goodbye!* filling the room.

Learn to Close the Sale

One day I had a revelation. The reason I was not making sales was because of myself, and nothing else. More specifically, I realized that it was my inability to ask for the order, to close the sale, that was causing me to be unproductive and unsuccessful.

The next day, in one of the sales books I was reading, I came across an explanation of closing and a specific closing technique. It seemed perfectly appropriate to my situation, where I was selling a simple item. It said that at the end of the sales conversation, customers know everything that they will ever know about your product. They do not need any more information, nor do they need to think it over to make a buying decision one way or the other.

Like a soldier marching into the guns of the enemy, I resolved that from then on I would force the sales conversation to a conclusion, one way or another.

On my first call the next morning, after I had made my presentation, the prospect said, "Well, let me think it over. Why don't you call me back?"

To which I replied firmly and confidently, "I don't make callbacks."

I still remember the prospect responding to me with surprise. "What do you mean, you don't make callbacks?"

I replied, "Mr. Prospect, this is not a big decision. You know everything you need to know at this moment to make a buying decision one way or another. There is nothing to think over. There is no point in me calling back, because there is nothing more to add. Why don't you just buy it?"

He looked at me for a few seconds and then said, "Well, if you don't make callbacks, I might as well buy it right now." He pulled out his checkbook, wrote the check, and pushed it across the desk to me. The sale was closed.

My Eyes Were Opened

I walked out of his office in a bit of a daze. I couldn't believe it. All those days and weeks that I had gone from door to door making my presentation, and making no sales, were solely because I had lacked both the courage and the ability to ask for the order.

I immediately called on the office next door, gave the same presentation, offered the exact same response when the customer said, "Why don't you call me back," and made another sale. Then I made a third sale, all within forty-five minutes. Whereas before, I had been making one or two sales a week, now I was making more sales in an hour than in a week.

From that day forward, I turned into a selling machine. I ran from door to door, from office to office, from prospect to prospect. My sales exploded. I started selling more in a day than half the sales force was selling in a week. I went from old clothes to new clothes. I went from a boardinghouse to an apartment. I went from taking the bus to driving my own car. I went from poor clothes to being much better dressed. Within a month, they made me the sales manager and asked me to teach everyone else what I was doing to make so many sales.

My point is that one sales closing technique that is appropriate for you at this time can transform your sales career. Not long ago, I had a sales veteran call me a month after he had attended one of my sales seminars to tell me that he had tripled his income in thirty days with one closing technique. This breakthrough came after thirteen years of selling his product. With this one new closing technique, which was perfectly appropriate for him and his market, he had tripled his sales. He taught this technique to everyone in his office and they all doubled their sales in the next month.

Why Closing Is Difficult

The close of the sale is the most stressful part of the sales conversation for both the salesperson and the customer. All customers have had negative buying experiences. They have bought something and found out later that they paid too much, that they could have gotten a similar or better item for the same or a lower price. They have purchased the wrong item that did not do what they expected it to, and eventually they had to replace it with a different product. After they bought it, they found the item for sale cheaper elsewhere. The item broke down and they could not get it repaired. They bought something they thought was a good idea and learned immediately afterward that it was a second-class product.

Every person has the fear of failure to some degree. Because customers have made so many buying mistakes in the past, throughout their lifetimes, they have an automatic fear of failure that is triggered whenever they are approached by a salesperson or sales offer of any kind. The fear of failure is 80 percent of the reason customers avoid making a buying decision.

On the other hand, the fear of rejection accounts for 80 percent of the reason the salesperson does not ask for the order. Most people are concerned about the opinions and feelings of others. This is what makes civilized society possible. But in sales, being overly concerned with whether the prospect will like you or approve of you leads salespeople to hesitate to ask people to buy their product.

Fully 50 percent of all sales conversations end without the salesperson asking for a commitment of any kind, even an agreement for a subsequent appointment to "advance" the sales process. The sales conversation simply ends with a "Thank you for coming in," and a "Thank you for your time," after which the salesperson departs, never to be seen again.

The New Model of Selling

In Chapter 4, we explained the new model of selling. This model gives you a blueprint for reducing the stress involved in closing for both the customer and the salesperson. It takes the focus of the sales conversation away from asking your customers to make a decision and instead focuses on how you can help those customers to improve their lives or work with what you are selling.

Building trust is 40 percent of the sales conversation. You build trust by taking the time to ask questions and to identify the needs of the customer carefully and thoroughly in advance. The more that you ask questions about what the customer's true needs, wants, and concerns are, and then listen intently to the answers, the more you build trust.

There is an inverse relationship between trust, on the one hand, and stress or fear on the part of the customer, on the other. The *higher* the level of trust and credibility you establish with the customer, the *lower* will be the fear, doubt, or concern of the customer when it comes to buying what you are selling. When the customer's trust and belief in you is at its maximum, the fear of buying your product or service disappears completely.

In the presentation, instead of trying to persuade the customer to buy something, you match the customer benefits of your offering with your customer's needs. You show that based on what the customer has said (people don't argue with their own information), your product or service is the ideal solution to the customer's problem or the very best way to satisfy the need in this area. By identifying needs carefully, and then by feeding those needs back to the customer in your sales conversation, the customer concludes for himself that your product or service is the best choice.

If you have built trust by identifying needs and have presented your product as the best choice based on those needs, then the confirming and closing—the final 10 percent of the sale—is much easier.

Conditions to Be Satisfied

There are four conditions that must be satisfied in the needs identification and presentation phases before you have earned the right to ask for the order:

1. The customer must *need* what you are selling. Your product or service will actually solve the problem or satisfy the need. Both you and the customer must be clear about understanding the need.

2. The customer can *use* what you are selling. You want customers to be able to get maximum value out of the product or service you are offering. You would not attempt to sell an expensive computer or a complex piece of software to a small-business owner who cannot use it at the level at which it was designed.

3. The customer can afford it. The customer has enough money to purchase the product or service you are offering without suffering. The value that the customer will enjoy from using your product or service must be clearly in excess of the amount you are charging.

4. The customer must actually *want* your product or service. Before you can ask for the order, the customer must have made this desire clear in some way. If you try to close the sale before the customer has given you a clear signal that he wants to buy what you are offering, you will often kill the sale, sometimes at the last moment.

How do you know that the customer needs what you are selling, can afford what you are selling, and actually wants what you are selling? Simple. The customer will say something that is quite clear—"It looks pretty good. How do I get it?" or "What's the next step?"—or otherwise give you a clear buying signal, such as leaning forward, becoming more positive and animated, picking up and holding on to your sales materials, or nodding and smiling at what you are saying.

If the customer does not give you a clear buying signal, there are two confirming questions you can ask to ascertain that the customer is ready for you to close the sale.

First, you can ask, "Do you have any questions or concerns that I haven't covered?" If the customer says "no," it means that she has reached a conclusion and is ready to buy or not buy. In this type of negative-answer question, a "no" may in fact mean, "Yes, I'm ready to proceed with the sale."

Second, you can ask, "Does this make sense to you so far?" In this case, if the customer says "yes," it means that he is ready to proceed with sale.

Sales Closing Techniques

There are more than a hundred different ways of closing the sale that have been identified over the decades. But at the end of the day, there are seven sales closing techniques that account for more than 90 percent of all closes. They are:

1. The Invitational Close

2. The Preference Close

3. The Directive Close

4. The Authorization Close

5. The Secondary Close

6. The Objection Close

7. The "Let Me Think It Over" Close

THE INVITATIONAL CLOSE

This close is simple and effective. At the end of the sales conversation you ask, "Does this make sense to you so far?"

When the customer says, "Yes, it looks pretty good," you reply by saying, "Well, then, why don't you give it a try?"

This question is actually two questions in one. The first part (*Why don't you...*) gives the prospect an opportunity to ask further questions or raise further concerns that he might have before making a decision. The second part of this close (... *give it a try*) invites the customer to take action and simultaneously implies that it is no big deal. After all, "You are just giving it a try." Even though "giving it a try" means that the customer is fully committed to buying and paying for your product or service, this question softens the decision, reduces stress, and makes it easier for the person to say "yes."

If you are selling services of some kind, you can ask, "If you like what I have shown you, why don't you give *us* a try?" When you say the word "us," you mean that your entire company or organization will put its arms around this customer and support the customer's need for the services.

If you are selling a hard product of any kind, you can say something such as, "If you like it, why don't you buy it?" Or, "If you like it, why don't you take it?"

Inviting the prospect to make a buying decision is a simple and yet powerful way to close the sale.

A friend of mine was a successful real estate agent (now retired). He told me that the day after my sales seminar, he was showing a house to a couple. When they came out of the house and back to the car, he turned to them and asked, "How do you like the house?"

The couple looked at each other and then at him and said that it seemed to be a fairly nice house. He then responded cheerfully, "Then why don't you buy it?"

The couple was a bit surprised. Apparently no one had ever asked them to buy a house before. They looked at each and then back at him and said, "Well, yes. Why not?"

My friend wrote up the offer on the trunk of his car right there in front of the house. He began to ask this question with every qualified buyer. His sales jumped 32 percent in the following month and continued to go up ever after. Within a few years, he was able to retire as one of the highest-paid salespeople in his industry.

The hardest part of learning a new sales closing technique is having the courage to try it out on a real live buyer. You have to summon up your courage and just blurt out the words for the first time. After that, you can use these words over and over, whenever it is appropriate. So, why don't you give it a try?

THE PREFERENCE CLOSE

With this closing technique, you give the customer a choice between one of two items: something and something *else* (rather than a choice between something or nothing).

You ask, for example, "Which of these do you prefer?" Sometimes this technique is called the "alternative close," because you present alternatives from which the customer chooses.

People like to be able to choose. People do not like an ultimatum, where they either buy or do not buy a single item. When you ask, "Which of these would you prefer, A or B?" the customer is much more likely to choose one or the other, instead of saying, "No, let me think about it."

If you only have a single product that you are selling, you can use the preference close on price, terms, or delivery. You can ask if people would like to pay cash or make monthly payments. You can ask if they prefer cash or credit card. "Would you like to take it with you today or have it delivered?" Whatever their answers to these choices, they have made the buying decision and you have closed the sale.

THE DIRECTIVE CLOSE

This is one of the most powerful closing techniques ever discovered. It has a 70 percent success rate with a qualified prospect. It is used by more salespeople in the top 10 percent of their fields than any other closing technique, especially in complex sales where the product or service involves serial factors and the sales relationship goes on well after the sale.

You ask the question, "Does this make sense so far?" If the customer says something like, "Yes, it looks pretty good," you then go on to wrap up the sale by saying, "Well, then, the next step is…" You then describe in detail the plan of action and the process of purchasing and taking possession of the product or service.

For example: "Well, then, the next step is that I will need your signature on these two forms, a check from you for $1,450, and the delivery address. I will take this information back to the office, complete the transaction, put it through our system, and the product should be delivered to you by Thursday afternoon, along with a complete explanation of our warrantee. How does that sound?"

In the directive close, you are "assuming the sale." You are acting as if the customer has already agreed, even though the customer has not really said "yes" to anything.

Sometimes this technique is called the "talking past the sale" close, because you talk as if the customer has already said, "Yes, I'll take it, what happens next?"

Using the directive close requires confidence, firmness, and directness on your part. Once you have used it a couple of times, you will find yourself using it over and over again, with great success.

THE AUTHORIZATION CLOSE

The authorization close is also quite powerful. It can be used at the end of a sales presentation by asking a question such as, "Do you have any questions or concerns that I haven't covered?" If the prospect says *no*, as you know, it means *yes*.

You then take out your order form or contract and fill it out, asking for the necessary details from the prospect. At the end, you then turn the contract around and say the magic words: "If you will just *authorize* this, we can get started right away."

You use the word "authorize" rather than the word "sign" because people like to authorize things but are often hesitant about signing things. If you ask people to sign a document, they can hesitate and ask you to give them some time to study the sales contract in greater detail and "think it over."

The Ultimatum Close. As another version of the authorization close, you use this technique when you have been going back and forth with a prospect for a long time and the prospect will not give you an answer, one way or another. The prospect always seems to want more information or more time to think it over. At a certain point, this prospect is draining you of time and energy. You have now invested so much time in the prospect that you do not want to lose your investment, but at the same time, this prospect is keeping you from calling on other prospects who may be better potential customers.

When you decide to issue an *ultimatum*, you call the prospect and tell him that you have more news for him that will be of interest. You tell him that you have something to show him and ask for a couple of minutes of his time in person. When you call back on the prospect, you have your order form filled out in every detail. You sit down and exchange pleasantries and then say something to this effect: "Mr. Prospect, I have given this a lot of thought. And either this is a good idea for you or it is not. But either way, let's make a decision today whether we are going ahead or not."

You then take out the completed contract and slide it across the desk. You say, "I have completed this sales order exactly as we have discussed it in the past, and if you will just authorize this, we can get started right away."

You then put a check mark where you want the prospect to "authorize it," smile, and sit perfectly still.

The rule is that whoever speaks first after asking a closing question loses.

When you push the contract across the desk, the prospect will realize that this is the last time that you are going to "call back." Either the prospect makes a buying decision or not, one way or another. It is "choose-up time."

In about 60 percent of cases, the prospect will look at you, look at the contract, look back at you, look again at the contract, and then finally say, "Okay. It's a good idea. Let's go ahead with it," and sign the contract, and you will have made the sale.

In about 40 percent of cases, based on extensive experience, the prospect will finally say, "No, I don't think it's a good idea for us at this time, but thank you for all of your efforts."

In any case, you are free. You have ended the back-and-forth of this inconclusive sales process and you can now go on to talking to new people and making new sales.

You should use this closing technique—this "sudden death close"—on a regular basis to clear your calendar and free up your time and energy so that you can develop new business. Otherwise, you can become bogged down with indecisive prospects who may never give you an answer one way or another.

THE SECONDARY CLOSE

Making a buying decision of any kind is stressful, and especially a buying decision involving a lot of money. To reduce the amount of stress involved in the buying decision, use the secondary close. You close on a *minor* issue of the product or service, the acceptance of which is a decision to buy the whole product.

For example, if you are selling an expensive automobile, you use the secondary close technique by saying, "By the way, if you were to buy this car today, would you want the factory tires or would you like the Michelin racing tires installed on your car?" If the prospect says, "Well, I would want the Michelin racing tires," he has decided to buy the car.

If you are selling a piece of software, you could say, "By the way, would you want us to install this software for you, or would your IT people want to do it instead?" If the customer answers, "We would like your company to install the software," or "Our IT group is quite capable of installing the software themselves," you have made the sale. You then go on by saying, "Well, then, the next step is that I will need your okay (or authorization), and then we can get started right away."

There are two factors that increase buying desire at the end of the sales conversation. The first is your willingness to take care of the details involved in closing the sales transaction, processing the order, and delivering the product or service. If you say, "The next step is"—describing the plan of action—"and I'll take care of all the details," you will dramatically increase the attractiveness of your product or service offering. It is amazing how many people hesitate purchasing a complex product or service because of time constraints. They are already overwhelmed with too much to do and too little time. Instead, always offer to "take care of all the details" for the customer. For example, you can say, "If you'll just sign the last two pages, I'll take care of all the details. I can fill in all the other information from our previous documents and get what I need from your accountant."

The second way to increase buying desire at the end of the sales conversation is to offer to "get started right away." Customers love the words "right away." Every time you say "right away" their buying temperature increases. Their desire to make a buying decision goes up. They start to think of the value, benefit, and enjoyment they will get from your product and are eager to get the process under way. In some cases, you will not be able to process the order and deliver the product immediately. But it is perfectly true that "we *can* get started right away!" This is a great motivation for the customer to make the buying decision immediately.

THE OBJECTION CLOSE

The prospect may say, "I like your offering, but we can't afford another $500 a month to pay for it." You then use the objection close. You say, "If we could spread the payments over an additional year and get them below $400 a month, would you take it?"

Sometimes this technique is called the "subjunctive close" because you use the words *could* and *would*. Neither of these words implies a commitment on your part. Both of these words leave the final action open-ended. For example:

Customer: We like your product, but we would need it by Friday and you require one month for fulfillment.

You: If we could get it for you by Friday, would you take it?

No matter what objection the customer gives you toward the end of the sales conversation, you always reply by saying, "If we *could* (answer the customer's concern), *would* you take it?" This forces the customer to say, "Yes, if you could do that for me, then I would make the purchase decision today."

Sometimes, the customer will say, "Well, yes. But we couldn't do it for this other reason." In this case, you use the same answer again. You say, "If we could take care of *that other reason* to your complete satisfaction, would you take it?"

When the customer finally says, "Yes, if you can do that for me, I will take it," you then say, "Let me see what we can do."

At this point, the customer has made a commitment to buy your product or service, but you have not made a commitment to comply with his final objection. In other words, the customer is on the hook, but you are not. You can now call your office, look into the situation, and confirm to the customer whether or not you can comply with his closing condition.

Objection or Condition. There are no sales without objections. (In fact, the previous chapter was devoted to this subject.) The existence of a single objection in the mind of the prospect can be enough to derail the sales process.

Here is an interesting discovery. When prospects raise an objection, they consider it to be a genuine reason for not proceeding with the sale. Because they do not understand that you have dealt with countless objections, and that you have considerable flexibility in taking care of your customers, they think that their objection means that they cannot go ahead, even if they want what you are selling.

This is why it is important to clearly distinguish between an *objection* and a *condition*. An objection is merely a concern in the customer's mind that causes her to hesitate about buying. A condition is a genuine reason why the sale cannot take place.

Customers may say they can't afford your offering, but often it's because they do not realize that you have a complete financing plan, including provisions to accept current products or services as a trade-in and to spread payments over two or three years. But when the prospect says, "I can't afford it," because her company has just gone into bankruptcy or has suffered a severe financial setback and is incapable of spending any money for any reason, this is a genuine condition that makes the sale impossible, at least at this time.

THE "LET ME THINK IT OVER" CLOSE

Throughout your sales career, no matter how attractive your product or service or how professional your presentation, customers will attempt to put off the stress of making a buying decision. One of the remarks you'll hear most frequently is, "Let me think it over. Let me think about it."

If you have qualified the customer properly, and you both understand that the customer can benefit from your offering in a cost-effective way, and the sale has reached the final stage, there is a 50 percent probability that the customer will buy today if you continue selling. In the other 50 percent of cases (and this is an arbitrary percentage), the customer cannot buy for reasons that have nothing to do with you.

When the customer says "Let me think about it," the customer is usually feeling stressed. Therefore, you do not argue. You simply smile, pause, and get the customer to relax by saying, "That's a good idea. This is an important decision."

You can even begin to put your sales materials away and close up your briefcase. Then, the customer won't feel under any pressure any longer to make a buying decision. When the customer relaxes and smiles, you then continue: "Obviously you have a good reason for wanting to think this over. Do you mind if I ask what it is? Is it the price?"

People are conditioned to respond when asked a question. You have now given the customer a choice about the reason he says he needs to think it over. "Is it the price?"

The prospect can answer in one of two ways. He can say, "Yes, it's the price," or he can say, "No, it's not the price." If price is the issue, then, fortunately, you have a complete toolbox of responses to a price objection. You can say:

- How do you mean?

- What do you mean, exactly?

- Why do you say that?

- Why do you feel that way?

- Is price your only concern?

- How far apart are we?

- You obviously have a good reason for being concerned about the price. Do you mind if I ask what that reason is?

In other words, if the prospect says that the price is the final sticking point, you have several ways to answer that objection, give a good reason to put price aside, and proceed with the sale.

What if the prospect says: "No, it's not the price"? In this case, you ask, "If it is not the price, then may I ask what it is?" In any conversation, a "May I ask?" question is very hard not to answer. Whenever somebody says "May I ask you a question?" you almost invariably say "yes."

When you ask and the customer gives you a response, you pause, carefully consider the response, and realize that you are on the verge of making or losing this sale. This is the final objection, or closing condition. Use all your advanced *listening* skills to ensure that the customer remains relaxed and that you remain in control.

After a pause, you then use the objection close and ask, "If we could handle that to your complete satisfaction, would you be prepared to go ahead with this offer?"

If the prospect says, "Yes, if you could handle that one last concern, we would be prepared to go ahead," then you reply with these important words: "What would it take to satisfy you on that point?"

You then wait silently for the answer. The only pressure you are allowed to use in a sales conversation, as a professional, is the pressure of the silence, which you employ after you have asked an important question, especially a closing question.

At this point, the customer will usually say, "Well, if you could just do this and this, we would be prepared to go ahead." You can then assure the customer, if possible, that you can do what the customer has just asked and go on to wrap up the sale.

Never Give Up

The most important word in closing the sale is the word "ask." Ask the customer to make a buying decision. Ask the customer if you can proceed to the next stage of the sale or the next meeting.

Ask confidently. Ask positively. Ask pleasantly. Ask courteously. Ask professionally. Ask cheerfully. Ask expectantly. But don't be afraid to ask.

At the very least, you can ask, "What would you like to do now?" This question by itself will very often lead to a buying decision.

One of my seminar graduates told me that he increased his sales and his income by 500 percent in twelve months with a simple technique. No matter what the customer said, positive or negative, he would always end by saying, "Why don't you just take it?" His customers might answer that "I don't want it; I don't need it; I can't use it; I can't afford it," or something to that effect. He would then respond, positively and expectantly, by saying, "Look, it's a good product. It's a good price. You can really benefit from it. Why don't you just take it?"

He was amazed to see how many reluctant or even negative prospects turned around and agreed to buy his product or service when he asked them one last time, "Why don't you give it a try?"

Courage Is the Key

The single most important quality in developing the skill of closing sales is the quality of courage. You develop courage through practice. *Boldness* is the key to sales success.

Take advantage of the "throwaway presentation." Whenever you talk to a prospect who apparently has no interest whatsoever in your product or service, you can either view the meeting as a waste of your time or you can decide to use a throwaway presentation on the prospect. You use the occasion to practice all your selling and closing techniques. Use every technique to uncover and answer objections. Ask for the order in every way possible. You have nothing to lose, and you might even be surprised. A completely uninterested or negative prospect can often turn around and become a customer if you persist in asking past the point where you are already convinced that you have no chance of making the sale.

Practice, Practice, Practice

You can only learn sales techniques, including closing techniques, by practicing them face-to-face with a real live prospect who has the power to buy or not to buy on the basis of your selling ability. You can role-play back at the office, or practice with your family, but the only way you can actually learn the skill permanently is by using it in front of a potential customer.

The wonderful thing about selling is that you cannot get worse at selling by doing it. And all selling skills are learnable. The more you practice these selling skills—especially the difficult, often stressful skill of asking for the order—the more calm, confident, and positive you will become and the more sales you will make. So, why don't you give them a try?

There is a sweet spot during the objection process when it is easiest to close the sale. At a certain point, your prospect will start stating objections and you will address them one at a time. At the end of this session, your prospect will start to run out of objections. You will notice longer periods of silence between when you finish your answer and your prospect is able to state another objection. Wait until there is an extended silence after your last answer, and then move to close the sale.

The best closing technique to use at this point is the "order form close." Begin doing something low-key, like filling out the order form or getting the prospect to answer a question about a detail such as a quantity, delivery, or launch date. With no strong objections remaining, the prospect will usually stop resisting and help you complete the order.

I like to imagine the objection portion of the sales process as an old-world sword fight. The two of you will begin full of energy, stating objections and answers confidently. But toward the end of this process, your prospect will start to become weary. You will have forced him to be on the attack for the first time in the sales process. Meanwhile, all your energy has been spent in a defensive posture merely reacting to his objections (attacks). Hang in there and your prospect will tire first. When his sword is down and he's panting for breath, that's when you close the sale and ride off into the sunset.

—MT

ACTION EXERCISES

Now, here are questions you can ask and answer to apply these ideas to your sales activities:

1. What are three major reasons for stress at the end of the sales conversation?

2. What are the three things you can do or say to reduce buyers' stress before you ask for the order?

3. What are three ways that you can build higher levels of trust in the sales conversation before you attempt to close the sale?

4. What are three things you must be sure of before you ask for the order?

5. What are the three best closing techniques discussed in this chapter for your product or service?

6. What are the two "confirming questions" that you must ask before you can close the sale?

7. What do you say when the customer says, "I want to think it over"?

Finally, what one action are you going to take immediately as a result of what you have learned in this chapter?

GETTING RESALES AND REFERRALS

What lies behind you and what lies in front of you,
pales in comparison to what lies inside you.
—Ralph Waldo Emerson

THE COST OF ACQUIRING a single customer today, especially in business-to-business selling, real estate, insurance, and in high-tech products, can be enormous. The expenses of time, travel, advertising, lead generation, presentations, proposals, and preparation can be hundreds and even thousands of dollars for a single customer. Acquiring a customer at this cost can put a company out of business unless that customer buys again and again, or becomes a dependable source of recommendations and referrals.

In selling today, we live in "recommendation nation." Your success as a salesperson will be largely determined by your ability to please your customers so well that they recommend you to others, over and over.

The very best salespeople, and the best companies, develop strategies to acquire customers and then keep them for life. Success depends on developing long-term customer relationships and then holding on to them in the face of ever more aggressive competition.

Your goal is to build a solid customer base of repeat sales. The best way is to become a "trusted adviser" to your customers so that once they buy from you, they come back and buy from you again and again, for as long as they need or use the product or service you sell. When you start every customer contact with the goal of both creating and keeping this customer for yourself and your company, you will treat the customer differently and be much more likely to achieve that goal.

Tougher to Sell

Customers today are tougher to sell to than ever before. When the economy is booming, customers buy much faster and with less thought. They are in a hurry, and they have the money to spend. But when economic activity declines, customer enthusiasm for anything new or expensive declines as well. Specifically, success in sales is more challenging because customers today:

■ *Are more knowledgeable about the products and services available to them.* They have more experience in using your product or service, or a competitor's product or service, than ever before. They are much more knowledgeable about their own specific wants, needs, and requirements. They set high standards with regard to quality, service, and value requirements.

■ *Are approached by your competitors on a continuing basis.* They are only one click away from every bit of information that has ever been written about your company, your product, and the industry overall. No matter what you offer, your competitor is willing to offer something similar, or often something better or cheaper.

▪ *Have more choices than ever before.* They can buy from you. They can buy from one of your many competitors. Or they can refuse to buy at all, at least in the short term. They have less urgency to make a decision. Whether they buy it today, tomorrow, or next year is often of little concern to them.

▪ *Are impatient.* If they have a genuine pressing need, people want immediate satisfaction. They want the product or service that you are offering immediately. If you cannot deliver the quality and quantity of product or service they require quickly after they have decided to buy it, they will hang up the phone and immediately contact your competitor who can deliver it faster. It is an unfortunate fact of modern business life that, if your potential customers find that you cannot satisfy their needs quickly, they will go to your competitor and never come back. You will never see or hear from those customers again. Your competitor will capture them "for life."

Achieving sales results today is harder than ever before. It requires more calls to find qualified prospects and then to get through to those qualified prospects. It requires more callbacks on qualified prospects to make individual sales. Customers are careful, cautious, and skeptical about buying; they need a lot of information and a good deal of reassurance before they can go ahead.

No matter what you sell, there is more competition for the business than ever before. Your competitors are aggressive and determined. They want the same business that you want and are willing to work as hard or harder than you to get it in the first place, and then to keep it.

The Second Sale

What is the purpose of a business? In Peter Drucker's great explanation, it is "to create and keep a customer."

Many people think that the purpose of a business is to make a profit. But a profit is merely the end result of cost-effectively creating and keeping customers. The very best businesses and the very best businesspeople think about customer creation every day, all day long. They're always asking, "What do we have to do to please and satisfy our customers better than any of our competitors?"

The first sale, creating the customer for the first time, is the most difficult and most expensive. The costs of customer acquisition, in terms of money, time, energy, and investment, can be enormous. Many companies actually go out of business because their cost of customer acquisition is higher than the net profit that they realize from making a sale to that customer.

Every week, you read stories in the financial press about companies that achieved billions of dollars in sales in a particular quarter or year but simultaneously lost hundreds of millions of dollars. How could that happen? How do companies achieve such high levels of sales and still lose money, and often go bankrupt or get taken over by rivals?

The answer is that their costs got out of control. They are paying too much to acquire customers relative to the amount of money they are actually earning from those customers. Because of high fixed costs, inefficiencies, excessive expenses for processes and procedures, and other factors, the company is "losing money on every sale, but planning to make it up on volume."

It is the second sale that is the most important in business. You can get the first sale with discounts, deceit, and false promises. You can induce customers to buy by ensuring them that they will enjoy benefits, outcomes, and results that are substantially in excess of the cost.

But the second sale is *proof* that you have delivered on the promises you made to get the first sale, in the first place. When the customer buys from you again, the customer is saying, in effect, "Thank you. You fulfilled your promises when I bought from you the first time. Now I am back to buy from you again."

This is why *resales* are as much as ten times easier than new sales. They require only one-tenth of the time and effort to achieve as going out into the marketplace and acquiring a new customer for the first time. Instead of having to advertise, contact prospects, make appointments with prospects, make presentations, negotiate contracts, arrange payment terms, and everything that is involved in a first sale, the second sale—the resale—is fast, easy, and inexpensive. This is why all successful companies and sales-people are focused on generating a continuous stream of resales from happy customers.

In addition, referrals from happy customers are *fifteen times* easier to sell to than cold calls. In comparison with finding brand-new customers for the first time, making a sale to a referral or recommendation requires only one-fifteenth of the time, energy, and expense. If one of your customers, who likes you and is happy with your product or service, hands you over to one of his friends or associates, the sale is 90 percent made when you walk in the door. As they say, "The sale is yours to lose."

Remember, customers are time-efficient (lazy) and always looking for ways to make decisions faster and easier. When someone they know and respect recommends a product or service, the entire process of evaluation and deliberation can be short-circuited completely. If your friend has bought a product, you can confidently buy the same product immediately.

In sum, customer retention is the key to sales success. Single-purchase customers are too hard and too expensive to acquire, especially if they only buy once and never buy again. Your focus in the first customer interaction must be on the second sale, and the third. Even before you make the first sale, you must be thinking about everything that you will need to do to make this customer so happy that he buys from you again and again.

Your first goal is to make a sale. Your second goal is to make resales to the same customer, over and over. And your third goal is to get referrals to new prospects from your satisfied customers. The purpose and goal of the company and the salesperson is as follows: "Get the customer to buy from you first, buy again, and then bring his friends."

Develop Customer Advocates

The most powerful sales and marketing influence in the market today is word of mouth. Fully 85 percent of the reason that a person consumes any product or service is because someone else has said that it is a good choice.

Human beings are inordinately influenced by the opinions of others, especially the opinions of people that they know, like, admire, and respect. Michael Jordan was paid $15 million a year to bounce a ball and shoot a basket wearing "Air Jordans." People go to the store and pay hundreds of dollars for those shoes because of the credibility attached to them because Michael Jordan wears them.

If friends of yours call you and tell you that they have just made a particular purchase, after carefully studying the pros and cons, and they are delighted with the results, you will immediately want to make the same purchase yourself. If a friend of yours tells you to go and see a popular movie, you will often go and see it that night. If a friend of yours tells you about a great restaurant, you will want to go to that restaurant immediately. If a person tells you about a "killer app" for your smartphone, you will probably download it right there, while you are still talking to your friend.

Word of mouth is very powerful. That is why your primary aim in selling, the highest level to which you can aspire, is to get your customers selling for you. This is called "customer advocacy." You achieve this goal when you take such good care of your customers that they want their friends and associates to enjoy the same experience they are enjoying by consuming and using your product. They also want to reward you in the spirit of reciprocity.

The key to customer advocacy, to widespread word of mouth, is not only having an excellent product, but also outstanding customer service. In the PIMS (Profit Impact of Marketing Strategy) studies, researchers found that the quality of a product, which is the critical determinant of repeat business, is made up of both the product itself and the associated services involved in delivering the product to the customer. The associated services also include how the customer is treated after the sale. The combination of the two, product and service, determines the total impression that the product and company make on the customer.

Serve Your Customers Quickly

One of the most important variables in excellent customer service is speed. Customers today, at all levels, have a "need for speed." Because of the halo effect—which says that if you have one positive quality, you create a halo that causes customers to believe that you have many positive qualities—speed can be the competitive advantage that allows you to leapfrog your competitors.

When a company takes care of us in a fast and efficient way, we automatically assume that company is *better* in every area than a company that responds to our needs slowly. We assume that a company that is fast and efficient also has better-quality products. They have better-quality people. Their products and services are actually worth more money than competitors whose services are slower. They have better people at all levels. Customers can sometimes go a little bit overboard just because you take care of them quickly when they have a problem or need.

For this reason, fast action on complaints is essential to your success in business. It has been found that if a customer complains, as many customers will over time, the speed at which you resolve the complaint determines the future of your relationship with that customer. If you move quickly to resolve the complaint and make the customer happy, the customer will actually be *more* loyal to you, and speak more highly about you, than if you responded to the complaint slowly and took care of it in a week or two.

Because of the complexity of modern products and services, there will always be problems and shortcomings that will lead to customer concerns and complaints. It's normal, natural, and unavoidable. The only factor that is under your control is how quickly you resolve complaints once they occur. When you move fast on a complaint, you make your customer happy. And happy customers are the ones who buy more and tell their friends.

Regular Follow-Up and Customer Contact

Once you have sold a product or service, regular follow-up and continuous customer contact are essential. Customers feel wonderful when you follow up with thank-you cards or e-mails, telephone calls to make sure that your customers have no questions, and regular visits. These actions make them feel valuable, important, and appreciated. It raises their self-esteem and makes them happy. When you deliberately do and say things that make your customers happy that they bought from you rather than from someone else, you "bind them to you with hoops of steel." You make them more loyal and dedicated to you and more likely to recommend you to their friends.

One of the recommendations we make to our clients is, at the beginning of the year, call back on every customer from the last twelve to twenty-four months and simply ask them, "Is there any way that we can help you or serve you today? Do you have any problems or concerns with the product or service we sold you last year?"

When salespeople do this kind of callback, especially at the beginning of a year or of a sales period, they are astonished at the feedback they receive. The positive reactions they trigger can be turned into subsequent sales conversations to make more sales. The negative feedback they receive creates opportunities to serve and satisfy the customer quickly, building loyalty and dedication.

How you phrase your customer service questions is important. If you ask, "How is everything," the customer will usually say, "Fine!"

When a customer says "fine," it often means that they are dissatisfied for some reason but they don't want to get into an argument with you. It usually means they are planning to move on to your competitor when they have finished using your current product or service. They are on their way out the door.

So instead, you ask the question, "How can we improve our services to you next time?"

The magic words are *next time*. Whenever you ask customers how you can serve them better the next time, in the future, they will always have one or more suggestions. These suggestions are their real complaints and concerns. If you can move immediately to resolve these complaints, you can build higher levels of customer loyalty than existed before.

Never ask, "How are things going?" Always ask, "How can we be of greater service to you next time? How can we improve our services to you in the future? Is there anything that we could do in the future to take better care of you?"

By Referral Only

The measure of your customer service success is the *percentage* of your business that comes from repeat sales and referrals. The most successful companies have a long-term goal to work "by referral only." They strive to take such good care of their customers that, once they have acquired a customer, they not only keep that customer for life, but they get all the friends and associates of that customer to buy from them as well.

Here is an exercise for you. Imagine that you could not prospect anymore. You could not go out and contact new people and make presentations. Instead, you would have to develop all of your new business from referrals—from calling back on your previous customers, taking excellent care of them, and getting referrals from them to new customers.

One of my clients was enjoying tremendous sales in a boom economy. The salespeople were highly incentivized to make sales but had little incentive to follow up after the sales. They turned the customers over to the company and it was the company's job to take care of them.

Although they were making a lot of sales, they started to receive a lot of customer complaints. Because of the lack of follow-up service from the salesperson, who had promised the moon, customers were becoming increasingly disenchanted. They were refusing to buy again or to recommend the company to others. Some of them were canceling their orders and going to competitors.

The executives of the company were quite concerned. They realized that they had set up an incentive system that paid people to make sales but did not pay them for regular follow-up service. So they decided to change the sales system and incentive structure.

At the beginning of December, they brought the sales force together and made an announcement. Effective January 1, there would be no more lead generation, cold-calling, or new customer development activities. From that date forward, each salesperson would be required to call back on customers from the last one or two years, make sure that they were completely satisfied with their services, and ask for referrals.

Many people in the sales force were furious. They were accustomed to making good money developing new business. Some of them threatened to quit if the company would no longer provide leads or they could no longer make new sales. And some of them did.

But on January 2, the remaining members of the sales force went out and began calling on each previous customer. They would sit down with their customers and carefully review every detail of the product or service installation, making sure that the customers were completely happy. When the customers expressed a complaint or concern, the salespeople promised to take care of it immediately, and they did.

At the end of each customer service visit, the salespeople would then ask, "Is there anyone else you might know who might be interested in our products and services as well?"

To their surprise, they found that their customers were a gold mine of recommendations and referrals. It seemed that every customer knew three, five, ten, or as many as twenty or thirty other companies or customers, in similar situations, who could take advantage of the company's products and services. The salespeople found that there was more potential business residing in their customers' Rolodexes than they had ever imagined.

In the following year, simply by calling back on existing customers and giving excellent customer service and attention, they uncovered a treasure trove of recommendations and referrals. The average sales of the company jumped 34 percent that year, and the salespeople in that company earned more money than they ever had before under the old system.

Treat Them As If You Could Lose Them

Imagine that you could not prospect anymore. What would you do to develop new business? By calling back on all your previous customers, you might be surprised to find out how much business you had overlooked.

The key is to treat every customer, every day, as if you were on the verge of losing that customer to your competitors. Imagine that every customer is sitting there looking at a proposal from one or more of your competitors and thinking about shifting business to that competitor and never coming back. If this was the case, especially with your most important customers, what would you do differently in your customer service activities?

Many years ago, I developed a close customer relationship with a company in Chicago. Over the years, in my travels, I would deliberately pass through Chicago to visit this customer, sometimes spending several hours with its senior executives, taking them out for dinner and offering ideas and advice on how to improve their business with my products and services.

Over the years, they steered more and more business to my company. My competitors were jealous. They were continually asking me how I was able to do so much business with this company, year after year. For a long time, I really did not know what to tell them.

Then, one day, at dinner with my clients, they told me the answer. They said, "The reason that we have done so much business with you over the years is because you are the only one of our suppliers who comes and visits us all the time. We see you almost every month, even though we know that you have to fly out of your way to come to Chicago. Because we see you so often, we feel very comfortable with you and prefer to do business with you rather than with your competitors."

Why Customers Defect

Your job is to create and keep a customer. Once you have created a customer, your goal must be to keep that customer indefinitely, for as long as the customer uses the product or service that you sell. This is the key to both business and sales success.

Just as you do everything possible to increase the customer's loyalty to you, you should simultaneously refrain from the behaviors, based on research, that lead to customer defection—to customers going away and never coming back.

The first reason customers stop buying and go somewhere else is because of the salesperson's lack of attention: The salesperson makes the sale, tosses it over his shoulder to the company to service, and goes on to the next customer. During the sales conversation, the salesperson is warm, positive, genial, and enthusiastic and promises an excellent product or service and a great sales relationship. But after the sale, the salesperson disappears and is often never seen again.

The second reason customers defect is *indifference* on the part of someone in the company. The customer calls with a question or concern, and the person taking the call obviously doesn't care at all. To avoid this situation, the best companies have the very best and most helpful people on the customer service desk. Remember, people are completely emotional. And emotions are triggered when they interact with another person. If your customers call someone who does not seem to "care" about them, they become offended and take their business elsewhere.

When a customer experiences indifference on the part of someone in your company, the customer feels devalued, demeaned, and diminished. The customer feels insulted that the company considers him and his business to be of little value. This experience offends the customer so much that he puts down the phone and says, "The hell with it!" and switches his business to your competitor—forever!

Respond Quickly to Customer Questions

Another reason for customer defection is lack of responsiveness to inquiries or questions. Remember we talked about the need for speed. If customers call your company with a question and nobody calls them back—promptly—customers can become irritated and agitated.

If customers are calling with questions or a problem, it is as if they are experiencing an immediate sharp pain. They are waiting for the company to take the pain away. Customers don't call to entertain themselves during the day. They call because they have a genuine need and trust the company to take care of them. If the company does not call back quickly, and act quickly, the pain may induce a customer to go somewhere else.

Very often this lack of responsiveness is to complaints of some kind. The prospect has a problem, or the company has not delivered on a promise that it made. The product or service is not working as it was supposed to. Customers call to express their complaint, and no one phones back or offers to resolve the complaint.

Many years ago I was doing a series of leadership seminars for IBM. Occasionally, the location of the seminar would change. Since I was flying 2,000 miles to Toronto to give these seminars, it was important for me to know exactly what hotel or facility the company had booked. Because of our busy schedules, one of the seminar locations "fell through the cracks." The organizers had failed to send me the exact address of the facility. It was the evening before I departed for Toronto, and I phoned from Western Canada to the offices of IBM to find out where to go when I arrived. It was about 8:00 p.m. in Toronto and the person who answered the phone was quite polite. I told him of my dilemma and named the executive I worked with and explained that I needed to get the correct address before I got on the plane. He said, "Don't worry. I'll take care of it and get back to you."

About fifteen minutes later the phone rang. The gentleman I had spoken with had collected the information that I needed. He had contacted the seminar organizer, gotten the address where the seminar would be held, and was passing it on to me. I thanked him profusely for his help. Then I asked, "By the way, it is now about eight-thirty at night in Toronto. You must be working awfully late."

I will never forget his response. He said, "Of course I'm working late. I'm the janitor, and I am cleaning up the offices."

Surprised, I asked him why it was that he would go out of his way to find this information for me if he was just the janitor. "At IBM," he said, "whoever answers the phone owns the problem."

Wow! I still remember that statement: "Whoever answers the phone owns the problem." That is the attitude of the truly exceptional individual and organization.

Remember, if a customer has a complaint or concern, a fast response builds loyalty. But a slow response triggers fear, anger, and can often drive the customer away forever.

The Ultimate Question

Develop an endless chain of referrals from satisfied customers. Once you have made a sale, take such good care of your customers that they would never think of buying from anyone else, even if another company offered a lower price or different features and benefits. Take such good care of customers that they want their friends and associates to enjoy the same experience that they are having with you and your company. Take such good care of those customers that they tell other prospective customers to buy from you continually, whenever they get a chance.

Turn each customer into a customer advocate. Get your customers selling for you everywhere they go, and to everyone with whom they speak who can use your product or service.

After many years developing customer service strategies for small and large companies, Fred Reichheld of Bain & Company wrote *The Ultimate Question*, a book that explains one of the most important breakthroughs in business success. What Reichheld and his associates found was that you can boil down all customer surveys, focus groups, and interviews regarding how customers feel about their suppliers into a single question: "Based on your experience with us, would you recommend us to others?"

They asked customers to rate their suppliers on a scale of 1 to 10 by answering this question. They found that customers that gave a 9 or 10 rating based on their experience with a company would represent 85 percent of that company's resales and new business. Customers who gave lower scores would represent increasingly less business, and customers who gave the lowest scores would be active "detractors." Not only would they not buy again from the company, but they would tell other people not to buy from this company as well.

The willingness of your customers to recommend you to another, to risk their credibility and personal reputation, is the highest level of customer satisfaction. When you use this question to organize your activities with your customers, you will significantly improve your customer service, almost overnight. At the same time, you will rapidly increase the number of recommendations and referrals that you get to other high-potential prospects and customers.

From now on, whenever you have had an interaction with a customer, simply ask, "On a scale of 1 to 10, how would you rate our service to you at this time?"

If the customer gives you any rating *less* than a 9 or 10, you smile and say, "Thank you very much for your answer. Please tell me, what would we have to do to get a score of 10 from you in the future?"

Surprisingly, your customers will tell you what you need to do to get a higher score. I teach salespeople over and over again that if you ask your customers for their feedback, your customers will make you rich. Your customers will make you successful and happy. They will tell you exactly what you need to do to get more of their business, and to get more of the business of other prospects. But you have to ask them.

Whatever your customer tells you that you would need to do to get a higher score, offer to do it *immediately*. In many cases, it will simply require better or faster customer service. It will require better or faster responses to customer concerns and complaints. Usually, what customers ask for is inexpensive and quite reasonable. And if you do what they ask, their loyalty to you will surge, like the mercury in a thermometer on a hot summer day.

The Relationship Selling Strategy

To ensure continual resales and referrals, focus on building rapport and trust from the first customer contact. Ask questions, listen closely to the answers, and position yourself as a trusted adviser to this prospect. Take the time to learn everything that you possibly can about the customer so that the customer knows you, likes you, and trusts you more than anyone else.

Take the time to build your credibility by explaining your personal competence and the competence of your company in satisfying the customer's needs and solving the customer's problems.

Develop a relationship maintenance strategy, even before you meet the customer for the first time. Take a piece of paper and write down a list of activities you will engage in, from the first sale onward, to ensure that this customer remains happy and satisfied and feels so good about you that the customer will recommend you willingly to other people. Remember, it takes one-fifteenth of the time, cost, and energy to sell to a referral as compared with a cold call or a customer that you generate through your lead acquisition activities.

Service your customers better than anyone else. Continually ask, "How can we serve you better? How can we improve our services to you in the future?"

And no matter what the customer says, always respond, "We will get on that right away!" Whenever you promise to do things right away, quickly, immediately for your customer, you build trust and credibility. You make customers feel happy that they chose you to buy from rather than someone else.

Develop a customer sales and service strategy that allows you to get and keep customers for life. This is the foundation of a great sales career and the foundation of all long-term business success.

Someone said that there may be a better rule for effective living than the Golden Rule, but no one has yet discovered it. The Golden Rule says, "Do unto others as you would have them do unto you." In selling and business, the application is simple: "Treat your customers the way you would like them to treat you if the situation was reversed."

In its simplest terms, the Golden Rule is the reason for business success. It's the reason for career success. It's the reason for personal success and happiness. It's the reason for success in family life. When you practice the Golden Rule with your prospects and customers, you will probably never make another mistake.

This customer service approach does not happen by accident. It requires careful planning, discussion, coordination, and training of everyone who deals with customers. There must be rewards and recognition for those who go the extra mile to please and satisfy customers. All successful salespeople and businesses are known for how well they treat their customers. This must be your goal as well.

Chapter 4 gives detailed steps on relationship building, including important aspects of a buyer's psychology to keep in mind for keeping the relationship after the sale.

Perhaps the most important rule in selling is to "sell unto your prospects as they want to be sold to." All people are different in their wants and needs and their ways of communicating and being communicated with. Take some time to find out if they are emotional or analytical.

Emotional buyers will be compelled by enthusiasm, conviction, and your personal energy. Analytical buyers will want you to convince them with empirical evidence, testimonials, and numbers. Listen to their questions and comments and be prepared to make adjustments to your presentation so that you can deliver a compelling case to both types.

Do everything to turn your customers into your champions. Occasionally, one of your customers will go out of his way to refer new business to you. The best way to encourage this behavior is to return the favor. Instead of waiting for your customers to step up, look for ways to refer business to your biggest accounts. The business you refer to others will result in more deposits into the "bank of reciprocity." Your account in this bank will always balance out to your benefit in additional business.

—MT

224 UNLIMITED SALES SUCCESS

ACTION EXERCISES

Now, here are some exercises and questions you can ask and answer to get more resales and referrals.

1. List three actions you can take with every customer to increase the customer's likelihood of buying from you again.

2. Why is it that second and third sales are more important than the first sale?

3. Why is it that resales and referrals are easier and more profitable than prospecting and new customer development?

4. Why is word of mouth so important in sales today?

5. How can you increase the amount of business that you get from referrals?

6. What are three reasons for customer defections?

7. How can you service your customers so well that they buy from you over and over again?

Finally, what one action are you going to take immediately as a result of what you have learned in this chapter?

TIME MANAGEMENT FOR SALES PROFESSIONALS

The ability to focus attention on important things is
the defining characteristic of intelligence.
—Robert J. Shiller

MORE THAN 100 years of research and countless millions of dollars have been invested in seeking the causes for success and failure in selling and in most other fields. At last, we have the answer.

It is simply this. People are highly paid because they spend more of their time doing things of higher value. People are underpaid because they spend more of their time doing things of lower value.

Salespeople who spend every minute of every day focusing on high-value activities eventually rise to the top of their fields and make both a lot of sales and a lot of money. Salespeople who waste their time in low-value activities seldom accomplish anything of importance, even if they represent the best companies with the best products in the best markets.

In this final chapter, you are going to learn how you can take the ideas in this book and use them at a high level to get more results and better results than you ever thought possible.

Focus on High-Value Customers

The Pareto principle, also known as the 80/20 rule, is the most important time management concept ever discovered, and especially in the field of professional selling. You should use this principle every day, in everything you do, as the basic organizing principle of your time.

The 80/20 rule says that 80 percent of the value of what you do will come from 20 percent of your activities. Twenty percent of your prospects will turn into 80 percent of your customers. Twenty percent of your customers will buy 80 percent of your products or services. Twenty percent of your customers will be responsible for 80 percent of your resales and referrals. It is always 80/20.

Rather than chasing after every prospect, like a dog chasing a passing car, you should divide your customers and prospects by value, or potential value.

- *High-value "A" customers or prospects.* They have the ability to buy a lot, and to buy again, and to refer other people to you to buy as well.

- *Medium-value "B" prospects or customers.* It's still important to contact them, but only after you have exhausted your "A" prospects and customers.

- *Low-value "C" prospects or customers.* Even if they do buy, they can only buy a small amount. They can only buy once. And they have little ability to send you references and referrals to other customers.

It is amazing to me how many salespeople (including myself when I was younger) spend so much time on low-value, no-value customers, using up much of their time and energy so that they have nothing left to seek out high-value customers and prospects.

Practice Creative Procrastination

Perhaps the greatest thief of time, and of life, is procrastination. It is continually putting off the hard, gritty work of selling, especially prospecting, by making all kinds of excuses for why you are not quite ready to go. Your ability to overcome procrastination will largely determine your success in life. If you continue to procrastinate, you basically have very little future in selling, or in any other field.

The fact, however, is that *everyone* procrastinates. High performers and low performers procrastinate. But the difference is that high performers procrastinate on low-value tasks, while low performers procrastinate on high-value tasks.

From now on, practice *creative procrastination*. Deliberately plan your day and decide on the things that you are going to procrastinate on. A very good example of creative procrastination is having a "Not-to-do list." Make a list of the things that you are not going to do until you have completed your most important and highest-value tasks.

The more that you procrastinate on low-value tasks, the more likely it is that you will get into the habit of working on only your higher-value tasks, all day long.

Your Job Description

The job description of a salesperson is the same as the purpose of a business. It is to create and keep customers. Your job is to go out into the marketplace and find customers initially, to sell to them, and then to take such good care of them that they buy from you again and again, and bring their friends.

You should spend 80 percent of your time *creating* customers and only 20 percent of your time keeping them. A study done at the University of Minneapolis some years ago examined the typical career path of most salespeople. The researchers observed that salespeople would start off their careers slowly, begin to make sales, get better and better, and then plateau and decline in their sales results.

What they found was that when a salesperson had no customers, he spent all his time prospecting. But once he made a few sales, he found it easier to call back on previous customers, for various reasons, rather than bear the harsh winds of rejection involved in prospecting for new customers.

Whatever you do, over and over, eventually becomes a habit. If you develop the habit of continually making PR calls on your previous customers, you soon develop the habit of not developing new business. You become more and more comfortable calling back on old customers rather than risking rejection by calling on new ones.

Every minute of every day, you should counter this natural tendency by asking yourself, "Where is my next sale coming from?" That's where you need to direct your efforts and that's what you should be doing all day long. Of course, it is important to give good customer service, but only in between your new business development activities.

Three Key Activities

The work of a salesperson has always consisted of three basic activities: *prospecting, presenting,* and *following up to close the sale.*

Prospecting means that you keep your sales funnel full by continually finding new potential customers. One of the best uses of your time is to spend the first ninety minutes of each day in prospecting—in new customer development activities. Do not check your e-mail, make telephone calls, drink coffee, or chat with your coworkers. Instead, at 8:30 or 9:00 a.m. sharp, put your head down and work for a solid ninety minutes in prospecting for new people to talk to.

Presenting is where the sale is actually made. The vast majority (95 percent) of sales presentations can be improved. Sometimes a simple, small change in your presentation can lead to a jump in your sales results. In the presentation, you show your customers that your product or service is the ideal solution for their problem or need. Your ability to do so largely determines your income.

After you have made an effective presentation, you must follow up and close the sale. As they say in golf, "You drive for show but you putt for dough." In selling, "putting" is when you close the sale, get the customer to agree to buy, and get a signed order or a contract with a check.

Applying the Pareto principle, you should spend 80 percent of your time prospecting and presenting, and only 20 percent of your time following up. And don't mix them up.

Don't fall into the trap of most salespeople (including myself many years ago) of continually calling back on a prospect who will not say yes and will not say no. "Indecisive" prospects keep you hanging on, spending more and more of your time, because you don't want to write off the amount of time you already invested in them.

Keep your focus on prospecting and presenting. In your new business development activities, you will find gaps of time that you can use to follow up with those customers who have not given you an answer, one way or the other.

When Are You Working?

Sales and marketing managers have done surveys to find out how much salespeople actually work in a typical day. In one survey, done in 1928, after following salespeople around with stopwatches, managers concluded that the average salesperson works ninety minutes per day, approximately one and one half hours out of eight. The rest of the time was spent hanging around the office, chatting with coworkers, going for lunch, and taking coffee breaks. (Today, we'd have to add working on the computer, checking messages, and traveling.)

Over the years, despite the benefit of intensive time management courses, inspirational and motivational speeches and seminars, and instruction in the most advanced time management systems, the average salesperson still works only ninety minutes per day, according to more recent studies done at Columbia University.

Whenever I share this number with salespeople, they always protest and deny that it applies to them. So then I ask them: "When are you actually working in the course of the day?"

You are only working when you are prospecting, presenting, and following up and closing. You are not working when you are driving to a sales call, drinking coffee, checking your e-mail, or going out to lunch with your friends. You are not working when you are sitting in the office, reading the paper, or preparing sales materials. These are all "warm-up activities." But they are not the real game.

You are only working when you are face-to-face with a qualified prospect. We call this "face time." Everything other than face-to-face, knee-to-knee, head-to-head, and heart-to-heart work with a real live genuine prospect is not working. It is merely warming up and warming down, like an athlete before and after the actual competition.

A Corporate Experience

In 2009, as the Great Recession swept across America, I was booked for a speaking engagement by a media conglomerate that sold advertising space in radio, newspaper, television, and other outlets. This large company had more than 200 salespeople.

The vice president of marketing told me the company expected a sales decline of about 30 percent that year. Reason? The market had slumped dramatically, customers were cutting back on advertising budgets, and the economy was in a slump. I asked him, "Why don't you set a goal to increase your sales by 30 percent instead of allowing yourself to accept that they are going to decline by 30 percent?"

I then went on to say, "After all, your salespeople are only working ninety minutes a day, about 20 percent of the time. If you could get them to work three hours per day, or 40 percent of their time, your sales would go up rather than down."

This vice president was smart and personable. He thought that was a great statistic, but he said it did not apply to his salespeople. He told me that they were all professionals with an average of more than ten years of experience, and they used their time efficiently and well every single day.

Nonetheless, we decided on a strategy. We decided that we would hand out stopwatches to everyone at the seminar and encourage the salespeople to keep accurate track of exactly the number of minutes they spent face-to-face with customers on an average day, and then to report back those numbers to the company at the end of the month.

The seminar went quite well. I explained these statistics and numbers to the sales professionals assembled. They all got their stopwatches, and they all agreed to report the exact number of minutes per day and per week that they spent face-to-face with customers.

About six weeks later, I got a phone call from the vice president. He was a little bit embarrassed to have to call, he said, but the company now had the sales reports back from all its salespeople. He said, "I was astounded, when I added up all the numbers, to find that the average salesperson in our company was actually working ninety minutes and forty-two seconds per day."

The Minutes Principle

To be successful in sales, you must implement the "minutes principle" into your sales activities. This principle says that only face-to-face minutes with prospects and customers count as selling minutes. When you increase the number of minutes you are spending face-to-face, you will increase your sales and your income. Because selling is based very much on the law of probabilities, or the law of averages, if you simply increase the number of minutes, you will and you must increase your level of sales.

You should also use a stopwatch to measure your current level of sales activity. A stopwatch will allow you to accumulate the time, because you can start it and stop it each time you go in to see a prospect or customer. At the end of a day or week, you will know how many minutes you were actually "working" during that time period. (The first time you take this measurement, it will come as a shock to you!)

Resolve immediately to increase the number of minutes you spend with customers by 10 percent a week, on average. If your average is 90 minutes per day right now, you would aim to spend 100 minutes next week. In the following week, you would increase your number of minutes to 110 minutes, and then 120, and then 135, and then 150, and then 165, and finally 180 minutes per week—double the average, within seven weeks.

Every salesperson I have ever shared this idea with has doubled his income within two months. Many salespeople, by reorganizing their time immediately, have been able to double the number of minutes they spend face-to-face with customers within a week. And their income doubles at the same time. They come up to me at my seminars, shaking their heads and saying, "I never realized how easy it was to double my income until I heard that principle. And it works every time."

If you work on increasing the number of minutes you spend face-to-face with customers each day, and simultaneously continue to upgrade your sales knowledge and skills, you will actually turbocharge your sales results and your income. It is not unusual for salespeople, even in a down market, to double their income in as little as thirty days with these simple strategies.

How to Increase Your Face Time

The starting point for doubling or tripling your sales is simply for you to double and triple the number of minutes that you spend face-to-face with qualified prospects. Plan your sales work geographically, to reduce traveling time. Cluster your calls in a certain area so that you can see more people with less time spent traveling.

Because of the fear of rejection, it is not uncommon for salespeople to plan their sales calls many miles apart, so that they can spend most of their day traveling to and from the prospects' offices. But top salespeople divide their sales territory into quadrants and then work in one of those quadrants all day. When a customer is available to be seen, they slot that customer into the specific quadrant in which they will be working on a specific day.

Start earlier in the day so that you can see more people. Make your first call by seven or eight in the morning if you possibly can. Very often, the best prospects are not available during the working day. But they are available before normal working hours or after normal working hours.

ARRANGE BREAKFAST MEETINGS

When you call a prospect, and the prospect is too busy to see you, invite the prospect to join you for breakfast at a restaurant close to her office or place of business. We have found that people may be booked for lunch, but no one is booked up for breakfast. In fact, when you invite people for breakfast, they will be both pleased and amused. Probably no one has suggested it before.

When you meet the prospect for breakfast, about an hour before the person starts work, deliberately refrain from talking about business. Ask personal and general questions. Ask about the current status of the person's business. Ask how the economy is affecting business and sales. But do not talk about your product or service at all. The whole purpose of inviting a person for breakfast is to establish trust. It is to build a friendly rapport between you. At the end of the breakfast, very often, the prospect will suggest that you get together in the office to discuss your product or service, even though you have not mentioned it at all up until now.

CALL BACK LATER

If the prospect does not offer to set up a subsequent appointment, call the prospect back in a couple of days, tell him how much you enjoyed the breakfast meeting, and tell him that you have some ideas for him that could greatly improve his business or personal life. Then ask for a few minutes to get together with him to share ideas.

This technique of calling early and/or inviting people for breakfast meetings is used by some of the highest-paid sales professionals in the world to see people who are otherwise unavailable and to build selling relationships that would otherwise be very difficult to begin.

WORK ONE HOUR LATER

To increase your face time, resolve to work one hour later. Offer to meet with decision makers after normal working hours. Especially when you are talking to business owners or to senior executives, you will find that they start earlier and work later than their staff. They may not be available during the day, but they're often available after 5:00 or 6:00 p.m.

Occasionally, the person you offer to meet with after work will suggest that you get together for a drink. Of course, you accept. But when you do get together for a drink, you absolutely refuse to talk about your product or service at all. Treat this time together as a pure "social opportunity." Use this time to develop a friendly relationship, to build rapport and trust.

Very often, after you have spent thirty to sixty minutes together at the end of a working day, the prospect will suggest that you get together at his office at a different time, when you can seriously discuss your product or service.

CONTROL YOUR ACTIVITIES

The fact is that in selling, you cannot predict where your next sale will come from. People buy or don't buy for a variety of reasons, some of those reasons having to do with you and your product, and some of them having to do with factors over which you have no control.

You must, therefore, focus on what you *can* control, and that is the sales activities that you engage in each day. You can control yourself and what you do from eight in the morning until six o'clock in the evening. And by controlling yourself and your activities, which are directly under your control, you can control your sales results, which are only indirectly under your control.

Sales activities are controllable, while sales themselves are not. When you do certain things, you increase the probabilities that you will make sales. Play the averages in your sales work. The quantity and frequency of contacts largely determines the quality and volume of your sales results. If you speak to more people and see more people, you will create the opportunities to make more and better presentations, your skill level will increase, and your sales and income will go up. This is a matter of logic, a matter of law, and it is completely under your control.

One of the best definitions of time management is "control over the sequence of events." In time management, by setting priorities, you can decide what you do first, what you do second, and what you don't do at all. You are always free to choose the sequence of events in your working life. And by choosing the proper sequence, by doing the most important things first, you indirectly control your level of sales and the height of your income.

STAY ON TRACK

Here's the key time management question: "Is what I am doing right now leading to a sale?" If what you are doing right now is not leading to a sale, slam on the brakes and stop doing it immediately.

Remember, when you work for a salary or a wage, you get paid just for "showing up." But when you work in sales, you only get paid for getting sales results. You don't get paid for "playing nice with the other kids" at work. You don't get paid for coming in on time and not leaving until the end of the day. You only get paid for making sales, and your total focus must be on making sales.

In selling, the more people you see, the better you get. The more people you see, the more sales experience you get, which raises your level of competence. You get better every day.

The higher your level of sales activity, the more energy you have. The more people you see and talk to, the more sales you will make. The more sales you make, the more motivated you will be to call on even more people and make even more sales. Your career goes into an upward spiral of increasing success, day after day.

There are four questions that you should ask and answer for yourself every day, all day long, to keep yourself focused and on track:

1. *What are my highest value-added activities?* This answer is easy. Your highest and most valuable activities are prospecting, presenting, and then following up and closing the sale. You should be spending 80 percent of your time on these activities, every single day.

2. *Why am I on the payroll?* Imagine your child were to ask you, "Mommy/Daddy, why do they pay you money where you work?" What would you say? In all honesty, you would have to say, "They pay me for making sales. My income is determined by the number of sales I make, and the size of each sale." Asking and answering this question for yourself will keep you focused and on track.

3. *What can I, and only I, do that, if done well, will make a real difference?* This is one of the very best questions for personal management. Every day, and every hour of every day, there are tasks that only you can do. If you don't do them, no one else will. If these tasks are done well by you, they will make a real difference to yourself and your future. Sometimes these tasks include prospecting and finding new people to talk to. They involve upgrading your knowledge and skills so that when you see the prospects you have uncovered, you are excellent in every part of the sales process. Sometimes these activities that only you can do involve planning your day and organizing your time for maximum output.

4. *What is the most valuable use of my time right now?* This is the granddaddy question of time management. All the time management

books and studies in the world are aimed at one simple task. It is to help you to identify your most important task, and then to help you to get organized, get started, and complete that task before you do anything else. Whatever your answer to this question, be sure that what you are doing at the moment has value and that you will do nothing else until it is complete.

Become a student of time management. Read the books, listen to the audio programs, and take the courses and workshops. The quality of your time management determines the quality of your life.

Don't waste time. Get away from people who are time-wasters. Get out of the office and stay out of the office. Eat lunch quickly and drink coffee on the go.

From the time you start in the morning until the time you quit, late in the day, resolve to *work all the time you work*. This decision alone will make you one of the most effective and highest-paid salespeople in your field in a very short period of time.

The Big Turnaround

Once upon a time, there was a sales branch of a Fortune 500 company that was consistently ranked as the company's poorest-performing branch in the world. Out of 2,000 offices, it was consistently number 2,000 in sales productivity and performance, even though it was located in a large, prosperous city.

One day, in desperation, the company brought in a sales manager from the West Coast to turn the office around, even though previous sales managers had all failed. The company sent out an announcement to the salespeople that the new sales manager would be arriving in the office for the first time on Monday morning at eight o'clock, and everyone was expected to be there for the sales meeting.

At eight o'clock on Monday morning, the salespeople began straggling in, carrying their cups of coffee, talking, making jokes. By 8:15 a.m., most of the sales force had assembled.

The new sales manager introduced himself to each person, having learned and memorized their names, and then convened the sales meeting. He opened up with a question: "What is it that you *don't* see in this office?"

The salespeople looked around and back and forth, not sure what he was referring to. He then said, "You don't see any *customers* in this office. Your job is to call on customers. Therefore, if there are no customers in this office, you should not be in this office, either."

Then he stood up and announced, "This sales meeting is now over. I want everybody out of the office and calling on customers for the rest of the day. Thank you very much." Politely but persuasively, he whisked everybody out of the office, into the hallway and the elevator.

The salespeople were shocked. They were used to spending the first half of Monday talking about their weekends and the different games that had been on television. Now, without warning, they were back in the building lobby. What should they do?

Some of them said, "The heck with this, I'm going across the street to finish my coffee." Others said, "What the heck, we have enough sales leads, I'm going to go out and start calling on customers."

The next day, when they returned for the 8:00 a.m. sales meeting, they walked into the office and found that all of their desks and chairs were gone. There was no place to sit. The sales manager conducted the sales meeting standing up, saying, "Since there are no customers in this office, and your job is to spend time with customers, I have sold off all the chairs and desks because you won't need them anymore. We have put some desks and chairs in a couple of small offices in case you bring a customer to the office, but other than that, I expect you to be out seeing customers all day long. Have a good day."

The sales meeting now over, he stood there and waited until everyone left and went back out to work.

Of the thirty-two salespeople working in that office, ten refused to accept the new regime. They quit and got other jobs that were probably much easier. The twenty-two who were left went out and began to call on customers and make sales, and even more sales. The more sales they made, the more positive and motivated they became.

Within six months, that branch began to move up in the sales comparisons with other branches. By the end of the year, it was number 1,000 out of 2,000 branches. By the end of two years, it was in the top ten, and by the end of three years, it was the number one sales branch in the world for that Fortune 500 company.

The reason was simple. The sales manager, who became a star in the industry, had a very simple formula: Insist that the salespeople go out and engage face-to-face with customers all day long. Everything else will take care of itself. And it did.

You Determine Your Own Success

Remember, you are the president of your own personal sales corporation. You are the president of a company with one employee—yourself. You are responsible for selling one product, your personal services. Your rewards are solely determined by your *results*—your personal level of sales. You do not need to wait for someone else to come and tell you to go out and spend face-to-face time with customers. You can make that decision by yourself, and practice it over and over until it becomes a habit and it's automatic and easy. By focusing on making sales, you will soon become one of the great salespeople of your generation.

*In his excellent book **The Checklist Manifesto**, Atul Gawande describes how the top people in every field use checklists to manage complex tasks. Professionals such as engineers, doctors, and pilots all use checklists to reduce errors, increase productivity, and increase efficiency.*

Sales professionals as well can benefit greatly from using the checklist as a battle-tested time management tool.

Create five checklists:

- *Yearly Action Items*

- *Quarterly Action Items*

- *Monthly Action Items*

- *Weekly Action Items*

- *Daily Action Items*

Once you create your yearly checklist, reference it to create your quarterly checklist. Use your quarterly checklist to create your weekly list and your weekly list to create a list every workday. Follow these lists, especially your daily lists, all the time. You can significantly increase productivity and reduce stress by keeping on track every day. Use a checklist to plan your work and work your plan. It is one of the best time management tools ever discovered.

—MT

ACTION EXERCISES

Now, here are some key questions to help you set actions to get your time and your sales life under control:

1. What are the three most important determinants of your income?

2. What are the three benefits of becoming excellent in your key result areas in selling?

3. In what three areas of activity should you apply the 80/20 rule to your current selling activities?

4. What are the three most important things you do that determine how much money you earn?

5. What are the three most important things you can do each day to maximize your sales and income?

6. What are the three times in the day when you are actually working?

7. What three things can you change in your sales work to increase the amount of time you spend working each day?

Finally, what one action are you going to take immediately as a result of what you have learned in this chapter?

THE SEVEN SECRETS TO SUCCESS IN SELLING

YOU HAVE THE ABILITY, right now, to earn two and three times as much as you are earning today. Everyone who is *ahead* of you in the game of life was once behind you, sometimes far *behind* you. And what they have done to move ahead, you can do as well.

Here are seven final ideas for you to use every day to dramatically increase your sales results.

1. *Get serious about your work.* Make a decision to go all the way to the top, to join the top 10 percent in your field. Anything less than a commitment to excellence is an unconscious acceptance of mediocrity, of average or below-average performance. When you get serious about selling and make a decision to be the best at what you do, your life begins to change and you are on your way to becoming one of the top people in your profession.

2. *Identify your limiting skill to sales success.* What one skill, if you developed and did it in an excellent fashion, would help you to double your sales and double your income?

Whatever your answer, write it down, make a list of all the things that you can do to learn that skill, and begin today, one step at a time, to master that skill. You could be only *one skill away* from doubling your income. And when you have mastered this one skill (which you certainly will if you persist), you must then ask the question again: "Now, what one skill would help me the most to increase my income?" You then set that new skill as a goal, make a plan to learn that skill (including reading, listening, and practicing in this area), and then get busy.

For the rest of your career, become a do-it-to-yourself project, always working to develop the skill that can help you the most at that time.

3. *Choose your friends carefully.* Get around the right people. Charlie Jones used to say that "you will be in five years the same person you are today, except for the books you read and the people you meet."

Positive people associate with other positive people. Winners associate with winners. When you change your thinking and become a total optimist about yourself and your potential, you will begin attracting into your life other people who think and feel the same way.

Simultaneously, negative and unhelpful people will drift away from you, finding you to no longer be of interest to them.

Top salespeople are "loners." I don't mean that they are "a-loners," antisocial people who have no friends or associates. This just means that top people are selective about the people they associate with. They do not allow themselves to spend time around negative people who can drag them down with their complaining and their pessimism.

4. *Decide to live forever.* Take excellent care of your physical health. Make a decision today that you are going to live to age 90 or more. Then examine your current health habits and ask yourself, "What one health habit, if I were to develop it, would most help me to improve my levels of fitness and energy today?"

Determine your ideal weight and then make a plan to achieve that weight, and keep it for the rest of your life. Determine the level of physical fitness and energy you would like to enjoy, and then begin exercising on a regular basis so that you feel terrific about yourself.

Remember the 100-year-old man who was interviewed by the newspaper and asked how he felt upon reaching 100 years of age. He said, "If I had known that I was going to live this long, I would have taken much better care of myself."

Your job is to take excellent care of yourself today so that you do live that long, and you feel great about yourself the whole way.

5. *Practice creative visualization.* Visualize yourself continually as the very best in your field. Remember, the person you "see" is the person that you will "be." All improvement in your life begins with an improvement in your mental picture of yourself. When you visualize and see yourself as calm, confident, positive, and successful, your subconscious mind accepts that picture as a command and organizes your external behavior so that it is consistent with your inner picture.

You change your outside life from the inside, by creating exciting mental pictures of the person you would like to be and the life you would like to live.

6. *Practice positive self-talk.* Talk to yourself positively. Control your inner dialogue. Your emotions are largely determined by the way you talk to yourself throughout the day. Psychologists call it your "explanatory style."

The challenge is that if you do not deliberately talk to yourself in a positive way, you will automatically slip into thinking about things that make you mad or sad. Instead of letting this happen, say positive things to yourself, such as:

1. "I like myself!"

2. "I'm the best!"

3. "I love my work!"

4. "I can do it!"

5. "Every day, in every way, I am getting better and better."

The most powerful words in the world are the words that you say to yourself and believe. When you repeat these positive messages, over and over, you program them deeper and deeper into your subconscious mind until you walk, talk, think, and feel consistent with these words and thoughts.

7. *Get going and keep going.* Always take positive action: Get going, get busy, get moving, and develop a "sense of urgency."

The common characteristic of all successful people in all fields is that they are intensely action-oriented. They are in constant motion. They believe in "doing it, fixing it, trying it!"

The good news is that, the faster you move, the more ground you cover. The faster you move, the more people you see. The more people you see, the more sales you make. The more sales you make, the more money you earn. The more money you earn, the more positive and motivated you are to see even more people, to make even more sales, and to make even more money.

Keep repeating to yourself the magic words "Do it now! Do it now! Do it now!" until these words become programmed into your thoughts and feelings. As Albert Einstein said, "Nothing happens until something moves." Your job is to move. Be sure that you are the fastest-moving person in your sales team—the one who is in continuous action.

This is a wonderful time to be alive for excellent salespeople. When you become excellent at what you do, you will always be able to control your present and your future. You will always be able to earn an excellent living for yourself and your family. You will always be able to keep control of your own life and your own destiny.

Go for it!

INDEX

21ˢᵀ CENTURY SALES TRAINING
FOR ELITE PERFORMANCE

Learn How To Double Your Sales In 35 Weeks Starting Now!

In my FREE 3-part video training series I will teach you exactly how top producers earn 10 times more than the average salesperson and how you can become a leader in your sales industry.

In this 3-part video training series, you will discover:

- The number one thing that makes or breaks a sale and accounts for 80% of every deal! (HINT: it's not the product, price, presentation or even your sales skills!)
- The 5 key differences between average sales people and top salespeople who sell more, close more, and earn more money.
- The 2 most important minutes in every sale and how to use them to close deals.
- 11 words you must memorize and repeat to yourself every morning to become a master in sales.
- The 3 characteristics of top salespeople and how you can become one, too.

These sales strategies have doubled, tripled and even 10X'd the commissions for sales people around the world!

Get this FREE 3-part video training series here:
http://www.briantracy.com/SalesResources

12-Step Goal-Setting Process Plus Exercise

In planning for success you always start with yourself and your personal goals. Your work and your business life are what you do so you can enjoy the most important parts of your life – your family and your relationships.

This 12-Step Goal-Setting Process and Goal-Setting Exercise will help you determine what is really important to you so that you can make better decisions in your business and personal life.

Download the "12 Step Goal Setting Process" here: http://www.briantracy.com/SalesResources

Become a Certified Sales Trainer

A PROVEN 3-Step Process for Becoming One of the Highest Paid Sales People in the World

ATTENTION SALES PROFESSIONALS:

This is a lucrative business opportunity to market, sell and deliver a proven sales training process in demand by more than 15 million customers, and earn upwards of $10,000–$20,000 per month!

If you are a sales professional or a sales manager, then you have all you need to tap into this huge, hungry market that will pay dearly for your services.

There are over 15 million sales people and entrepreneurs that lay awake at night thinking about sales. They don't have the excellent sales training they so desperately need in today's competitive marketplace.

In this 3-part video training series you will discover:

- The ONE THING that has 15 million or more business owners going, "I NEED that…!"
- An opportunity for sales professionals to potentially earn 5 FIGURES a month by filling that need—doing something that you are already good at!
- How you can take control of your own TIME and FREEDOM—so you never have a boss again!
- How to focus and concentrate on the most important things that you can do that will lead you towards your goals.
- A 3-step PROVEN Sales process—it works everywhere, for everyone, in every business, under ALL conditions!
- How to develop a complete action plan for success that will propel you towards living out your dreams.

What I am going to share with you during this FREE 3-PART TRAINING could be the answers you're looking for and transform your life.

Get this FREE 3-part video training series here: www.briantracy.com/salestrainer

Brian Tracy is a professional speaker, trainer, seminar leader, and consultant and is the chairman of Brian Tracy International, a training and consulting company based in Solana Beach, California. He is also a self-made millionaire.

Brian learned his lessons the hard way. He left high school without graduating and worked as a laborer for several years. In his mid-twenties he became a salesman and began his climb up the business ladder. Year by year, studying and applying every idea, method, and technique he could find, he worked his way up to become chief operating officer of a $276-million development company.

In 1981 he began teaching his success principles in talks and seminars around the country. Today, his books, audio programs, and video seminars have been translated into 38 languages and are used in 55 countries.

He is the bestselling author of more than fifty books, including *Maximum Achievement, Advanced Selling Strategies, Focal Point,* and *The 100 Absolutely Unbreakable Laws of Business Success*. He has written and produced more than 500 audio and video learning programs that are used worldwide.

Michael Tracy is currently the Vice President of Sales and Business Development at Analog Analytics, a Software-as-a-Service company that was acquired by Barclays Plc in May 2012. Michael's experience also includes founding an online performance marketing company and managing door-to-door sales teams for AT&T and Verizon.

Other titles by Brian Tracy available in ebook format:

The Brian Tracy Success Library:
Motivation ISBN: 978-08144-33126

The Brian Tracy Success Library:
Delegation & Supervision ISBN: 978-08144-33157

The Brian Tracy Success Library:
Negotiation ISBN: 978-08144-33195

Crunch Point ISBN: 978-08144-30132

Focal Point ISBN: 9780-8144-26258

Full Engagement ISBN: 978-08144-16907

How the Best Leaders Lead ISBN: 978-08144-14354

Now, Build a Great Business ISBN: 978-08144-16983

The Power of Charm ISBN: 978-08144-29716

Reinvention ISBN: 978-08144-13470

Speak to Win ISBN: 978-08144-01828

Time Power ISBN: 978-08144-27859

TurboStrategy ISBN: 978-08144-29303

For more information, please visit: www.amacombooks.org

To learn more about Brian Tracy visit his website:
http://www.briantracy.com/